P9-CMO-815

Morality and the Mass Media

Morality and the MASS MEDIA

Kyle Haselden

BROADMAN PRESS
Nashville, Tennessee

To my brother, Clyde

422-345

Second Printing

Dewey Decimal classification number: 261.8

Library of Congress catalog card number: 68-20676

Printed in the United States of America

2.5AT6813

Foreword

Morality and the Mass Media is a very significant book by an author uniquely qualified to write it. Clearly, and with profound theological insight, Kyle Haselden focuses here on a subject of overwhelming importance. His own marvelously authentic Christian experience is combined with decades of social awareness and relevant ministry to produce in the first two chapters the finest rethinking of morality that I have found. Both ancient heresies and modern fads are mercilessly exposed to God's truth in a Christian spirit. Biblical perception, psychological understanding, a sense of moral history, a finely honed feeling for the nature of man, and a most uncommon common sense have all been skilfully woven together to present the case for Christian morality.

Then, with an equal passion for excellence, Dr. Haselden introduces the complex issues surrounding the mass media. After analyzing what is happening to modern man because of the mass media, he proceeds to a most informative probing of the whole field of mass communication. A brilliant searchlight is turned, chapter by chapter, on censorship, obscenity, radio and television, advertising, motion pictures, and legislation. Thoughtful Christians will find in these chapters a wealth of carefully researched material and a consistent commitment to understand the demands of Christian morality in each of these important areas. Among the most critical moral problems confronting modern man are those that relate to these specific topics.

The need for such a book has been clear for years. Accentuating that need are several significant developments that have accompanied the advent of the mass media: the population explosion which is providing ever growing masses of people over the whole earth; the continuing technological revolution which never ceases to unveil new mass communications devices ranging from transistor radios to orbiting satellites; the revolution in work, leisure, free time, extended vacations, and early retirement which guarantees the time to absorb the manifold messages of the mass media; and the growth of increasingly powerful national states which are especially tempted to manipulate the masses with the instantaneous media now available.

The timeliness of MORALITY AND THE MASS MEDIA is obvious.

I commend it heartily to pastors. Laymen will find it highly rewarding. Students will be stimulated by its brilliance. Study groups in churches will be challenged by it. All who believe that without an imminent moral imperative both culture and religion would disintegrate because of lack of ultimate seriousness will be encouraged and strengthened by carefully reading this book. It comes from a great mind, a great heart, and a great spirit for such a time as this.

FOY VALENTINE

Preface

As a Baptist minister and the editor of an ecumenical journal, it was inevitable that I should give considerable thought to the effect of the mass media on morality. Yet it had never occurred to me to attempt a book on this theme. I am therefore deeply indebted to Foy Valentine, executive secretary-treasurer of the Christian Life Commission of the Southern Baptist Convention, for the need and the opportunity to organize and record my thoughts on this subject.

With the exception of the two concluding parts, the chapters of this book were prepared, at Dr. Valentine's invitation, to be delivered as lectures to a conference sponsored by the Christian Life Commission at Ridgecrest, North Carolina, in August, 1967. Due to a sudden illness that prevented my appearing at Ridgecrest, Dr. Valentine had to serve not only as the inspiration for this series but also as its voice. The reader can therefore appreciate how deeply I am indebted to him for the production of this book, even though he is in no way responsible for the opinions I express here.

In addition, I am grateful to The Christian Century Foundation for my use of a number of quotations from articles and editorials in *The Christian Century;* and, to my secretary, Miss Elaine Kreis, for her efficient preparation of this manuscript.

Scripture quotations are from the Revised Standard Version.

KYLE HASELDEN

Contents

1
Rethinking Morality 11

2
Authentic Morality Defined 31

3
The Uses of Mass Media 51

4
Censorship and Morality's Habitat 79

5
Obscenity Beyond Sex 98

6
The People's Ether 119

7
Morality and Madison Avenue 140

8
This Barbaric Invasion 153

9
On Legislating Morals 171

10
Morality and the Sense of God's Presence 184

1
Rethinking Morality

The question confronting us asks in what way and to what extent mass media affect morality. This question cannot be properly raised—certainly cannot be adequately answered—unless from beginning to end the search rests on clear and acceptable definitions of morality and of mass media. Both of these subjects are cloudy—morality, because it is one of civilized man's oldest problems; and mass media, because this phrase describes one of man's latest accomplishments. If we are to gain some understanding of the new development's impact on the old concern, then we must have some fixed points to which our quest is related and by which it is continually corrected. Therefore we must spend whatever time is necessary clarifying our terms.

What do we mean by morality and by such commonly used terms as "morals," "moralism," "moralistic," "personal ethics," "social gospel," "the good life"? There are numerous ethical systems; can any one of them be declared exclusively Christian, or must several systems share that adjective? Does the new age in which we live, with its industrial, technological, secular, conurbated, impersonal society, require a moral code radically different from the one developed in a relatively simple agricultural setting? Is the new era in which we live changing the moral tone of the people whether or not we are willing to change the theoretical structures of morality? Have the media of universal and instantaneous communication helped produce for man a setting that outmodes old codes of personal righteousness, not only demolishing our inherited ethical systems, but also radically transforming man's character?

Has mass communication produced a climate in which man will inevitably become a different creature from what he has been in the past? If so, will the new creature be better than the old? What do we mean by "better"? If such a change occurs, to what extent will it be due to the new forms of communication and to what extent to the content presented by the new forms?

Our answers to such questions as these obviously depend on what we mean by morality and on our understanding of the nature and power of mass media. Therefore, we begin by defining the two parts of our general theme, morality and mass media.

The Extremities of Current Morality—Legalism

During the months in which this material was in preparation my thoughts about the meaning of morality swung between two poles so far apart that there seemed to be no connection between them. Neither of these extreme positions meets the demands the Christian faith makes on personal and social conduct, nor do we discover authentic morality by charting the middle ground between the two. Nevertheless, a description of the extremities of current morality will help us understand the importance and the difficulty of arriving at a common definition and may push us toward the answer we seek. Each of these approaches to the moral life deserves in any event an accurate and fair description if the two positions are to be seen in instructive contrast. The first of these extremes could be called Christian legalism; the second could be called Christian relativism, but is more popularly known today as "the new morality."

Christian legalism—the more popular of the two positions—assumes that in the teachings of Jesus and his disciples, in the Ten Commandments, and in the elaboration of these teachings and commandments in which church doctrines we have a detailed, inflexible, always appropriate, moral code which, in its minute prescriptions, is adequate for all times, places, persons, and circumstances. In this view the Christian has, so to speak, a "Robert's Rules of Christian Conduct" exhaustively indexed to meet all of life's contingencies. All that the Christian has to do, then, to meet life's complex moral demands is to learn these rules which have been imposed on man by an arbitrary God and rigorously obey them.

The legalist lives as though man were made by God to keep God's laws. The sacredness, that is, is in the laws; and the laws must therefore be honored and observed, whether they make any sense or not, whether they produce any benefits for man, or even if they are harmful to man.

Those of us who have visited Mea Shearin in the Israeli section of Jerusalem have seen an extreme example of this kind of legalism. In the part of Jerusalem called "The 100 Gates" a remnant of separatist Jews devote themselves to the minutiae of the law. They call themselves "the Watchers of the Walls." Although Jews, these people do not recognize the state of Israel, since its establishment was not preceded by the coming of a messiah. They refuse to use Hebrew in their daily life. To them, Hebrew is God's language, the specific word by which he created the universe and therefore one that must be reserved for God's law. These people have stoned cars driven through this part of Jerusalem on the Sabbath. The women do most of the work and the men spend as much time as possible in the synagogue reading the law.

The conditions in which they live, in sharp contrast to so much of the rest of Israel, are filthy. But to them life is a corridor, and the supreme duty of man while in the corridor is to keep the law. This, of course, is not Christian legalism. In fact, it is legalism at its worst. But this is the direction in which legalism moves. And Christian legalism sometimes moves in that direction.

The legalist lives as though Christ had not come to liberate man from bondage to the law. At his best and at his worst, the legalist is the rich young man saying, "All these I have observed." Yet he knows, even before Jesus makes the point, that there is an aching void in his legally perfect life. At the end he goes away sorrowful.

The legalist is the Pharisee, a good man, who in the Temple prayed, "God, I thank thee that I am not like other men, extortioners, unjust, adulterers, or even like this tax collector. I fast twice a week, I give tithes of all that I get." You see, he was telling the truth about himself: he was letter-perfect. Yet it was the other man who went down to his house justified.

The legalist is the group of scribes and Pharisees who brought to Jesus a woman taken in adultery and said to him, "Teacher, this woman has been caught in the act of adultery. Now in the law Moses commanded us to stone such." The legalist signs pledges and carries them for safety in his pocket, lest, without this talisman to finger now and then, he be tempted beyond his own strength and beyond the rescuing presence of God. The pledge card comforts him as the blanket does Linus. The power is not in him but in the blanket.

The legalist swears obedience by heaven and by earth, for, to him, the good life can be described in a manual which has no margins for venturesome faith.

Of course, there is another side, and I would be remiss if I did not mention it. In my fifty-four years I have known personally three, and only three, good men in the sense of consistent and, as far as I know, unfaltering righteousness. Each of these men would have to be described as in a sense legalistic. Each was pietistic. Each lived his admirable life by a code. Each subjected himself unreservedly to the discipline of that code. Each escaped the pitfalls of legalism. Each one of them, however, was committed to something deeper than his moral code, and it was this commitment rather than the code that gave righteousness to his life. This kind of personal discipline has to be praised, but note that in each of these cases the moral code was the product of a superior commitment.

Legalism usually goes wrong when it tries to create an internal condition by the application of multiplied external observances of externally imposed regulations. It goes wrong when it is conceived as a purchase on God and as a claim for prestige. Legalism has a penchant for veering in this direction.

In a sermon preached at the Rockefeller Chapel of the University of Chicago, and recently published in a book called *Rockefeller Chapel Sermons,* Theodore A. Gill gave a graphic indictment of Christian legalism. He said:

> It seems to me that for all too long a time it has been thought that the Christian life was a life lived within a legalistic box. The life that could fit within the boundaries of that box was a Christian life. The laws were the walls of the box; thou shalt, thou shalt not (two sides), thou shalt, thou shalt not (two sides), thou shalt

(bottom), thou shalt not (sealed top). There is the Christian life. You get inside the laws, you fit inside that box, and then you are living a Christian life. Whatever of you hangs out, whatever appetite or interest or urgency, whatever hangs out, whatever doesn't fit has to be lobbed off . . . chopped off. So the truncated life becomes the Christian life. The cut-off, the hacked at, the bruised and bleeding life—this becomes the Christian life. This has been the Christian life for too long a time for too many people in too many places.[1]

Even though Dr. Gill does not give us in this sermon an acceptable positive picture of the Christian life, he certainly knows what the Christian life is not. It is *not* legalism.

There are at least six reasons why legalism fails to qualify as authentic morality. First, legalism externalizes morality. A man becomes righteous by virtue of the laws he keeps; or, he becomes evil as a result of the laws he breaks. His reasons for keeping the laws or for breaking them are of no significance. He may refrain from murder because he is afraid, because he is physically incapable of murder, or because he prefers to torture his enemy rather than kill him. None of these restraints is commendable. But under legalism the important thing is that he has not murdered; therefore, he gets a mark to his credit. He refrains from fornication because he fears venereal disease, pregnancy, or public exposure. None of these motivations is moral. Under legalism the important thing is that he has obeyed a religious regulation against fornication; therefore, he gains another favorable mark. Or, he lies to save a friend the unnecessary and demolishing blow of some hideous truth. He lies, so to speak, in love. But the law against lying cares nothing about his motives. He has lied, has broken the law against lying, and therefore must be condemned. Obviously, by this scheme, which places the center of morality outside the person in a law that must be obeyed, we could with time and patience make saints out of well-trained monkeys.

Jesus, of course, repudiated externalized morality. He knew that adultery can be committed by a look, whether there is a physical act or not; that both the good and the evil which men do proceed

[1]D. E. Smucker (ed.), *Rockefeller Sermons of Recent Years* (Chicago: The University of Chicago Press, 1967).

from the inside out, rather than from the outside in; that man was not created so that God would have someone to keep the seventh day; that no amount of ceremonial handwashing could purify the soul; that one could keep all of the laws and still be estranged from God. Jesus relocated the center of morality from the statues worshiped by the Greek world and the statues worshiped by the Jewish world to the human heart. He knew and he declared the true inwardness of morality.

Second, legalism has to be repudiated as a Christian way of life because it describes the good life in static, restrictive, negative terms. In all legalistic codes, God's *no* tends to become louder and more repetitive than his *yes*. The law marks off in glaring signs the land of disobedience in which men should not travel, ever making that area of prohibition larger. But it does not open to the human spirit the vast, unexplored countries of joy, adventure, surprise, and service, which are the soul's true home. Thus God's "thou shalt not" obscures his gracious invitation, his exciting and inspiring challenge, his astounding trust. A palisade of *don't's*, of blindly and routinely obeyed prohibitives, turns the free man into a prisoner, the full man into a fraction, the questing man into a cautious scorekeeper. If, in the Decalogue, God came to a man as a restricting *no*, in Jesus Christ he came as a liberating *yes*. Legalism obscures this revelation.

This definition of morality as the restriction of human freedom has had an ancient and sometimes honorable history. It produced all that was best in the monastery and in the monastic life that has existed apart from the monastery—Puritanism, Protestantism's own monasticism, for example. This pattern of the good life can be presented most enticingly. Father Jan H. Walgrave, a Dominican priest, defined morality in restrictive terms in his contribution to the book *Moral Problems and Christian Personalism* (Paulist Press):

> Morality begins at the point where a man says to himself: "Although I can do this or that and feel inclined to do this rather than that, I do not wish to be pushed by whims or fickle emotions. I will let myself be guided by certain fixed rules which I feel myself bound by, or which I want to impose on myself." . . . Morality then is the norm or the totality of the norms to which freedom is subjected.

This, fortunately, was not all Father Walgrave had to say about morality. In time, I hope to show that authentic morality is exactly opposite to this definition. It is the freedom into which life is invited by Christ rather than the restrictions to which human freedom is subjected.

Third, legalism mechanizes morality. The moralist who lives his life by a rigid, arbitrary, prescribed code soon ceases to be a free moral agent and becomes an automaton. Like a programmed computer, the code-keeper operates according to a predetermined schedule. He obeys the laws and this obedience brings him into a relationship with them but not necessarily into a relationship with God. Since the morally perfect life, and not oneness with God, is his ultimate objective, his concentration on the law can in fact alienate him from God. But God does not want his child to be a flawless, faultless, smoothly operating machine; he wants him to be as a child who lovingly responds to a loving father.

Legalism eliminates the person as person. The vitality of such a morality is in the arbitrary code and not in the man; and the code, operating from outside the man, imposes on him a conduct which may be entirely arbitrary and which may in no way affect his fulfilment as a person. The individual's essential being, his "self," is displaced by an arbitrator who rules his life not from within but from beyond. This thought was well expressed by Charles B. Ketcham in the October 12, 1966, issue of *The Christian Century:* "Many men fear to live authentically, to be truly alive. The authority for their lives is simply turned over to another. For some of these, religion with its creeds, dogmas, and ritualistic rubrics pointing toward a tidy Kingdom fulfills this idolatrous function."

Fourth, legalism tends to concentrate on trivialities. I can illustrate this point best by referring to the moral code under which I was trained a half century ago in a rural area of South Carolina. Even though we did not attend church regularly—the mules needed their one day a week rest—there was a difference about Sunday that you could hear and taste. I still have a vivid recollection of my maternal grandfather, dressed in his only suit of clothes, sitting in a rocking chair on the front porch. He had the Bible on one side of him and a Sears and Roebuck catalog on the other. He alternately satisfied his spiritual hunger and whetted his sensual appetite as the slow day passed. That Bible and a mumbled grace at meals were the only formal evidences of religion in the home in which I was first taught the difference between right and wrong. But we considered ourselves a Christian people, a Baptist people. We had our moral code and by and large we lived by it.

The tone and essence of this code can be indicated by citing some of its specific regulations. It stated in part that good people do not swear, lie, steal, dance, play cards, drink whisky, or work on Sunday. It declared that good white people do not associate with Negroes and certainly not with mulattoes. It encouraged kindness to animals and respect for elders. As I look back on that code now, it was wrong, not so much because it laid down certain guidelines, but because the rules were negative, prohibitive, arbitrary, cluttered with trivialities, and—in regard to relations with nonwhites—blatantly immoral. Since the rules were not accompanied, and in some cases could not be justified, by logical, biblical, or practical explanations, they imposed on the child's mind and behavior arbitrary demands for blind obedience. Their net effect was therefore repressive.

Under such a system the child naturally assumed that goodness is equivalent to submission to external authority. Instead of opening the child's mind to the wonder, thrill, and beauty of life, the code locked it within a narrow area, circumscribed by commandments that, for good reasons, and no reasons at all, confined and cramped his free spirit. He became the code's puppet, moving only in response to strings attached to him externally and manipulated by hands other than his own.

The greatest offense produced by this code, however, did not come from the code's arbitrariness nor its externality. Rather, the gravest offense in this case resided in the fact that the legalistic system related the will of God and the thrill of the Christian life to the rejection of innocent pastimes. It taught that all social relations between Negroes and whites are immoral.

There would be no purpose in referring to the simple ethical system under which I was trained a half century ago were it not for the persistence of this legalistic, often superficial, sometimes immoral, ethical system among great numbers of American Christians. The items of the code may be different from those I was taught as a boy but the character of the code—arbitrary, repressive, trivial, and immoral—remains unchanged.

Needless to say, the legalistic demands today are not nearly so strict nor so detailed as they once were. But the philosophy underlying legalism still dominates the lives of numerous Christians. To them the good life is conformity to a set of prescribed regulations and the bad life is failure to comply with such regulations. And, in the main, the controlling regulations have little bearing on the life and death issues with which men struggle.

Fifth, when strictly observed as a way of life, legalism binds the future. No matter what the future may hold "of marvel or surprise," the legalist has already determined how he will meet it, not only the spirit *in* which he will meet it, but also the exact conduct *by* which he will meet it. He already has, so he believes, not only the principles but also the particulars for his future behavior. He enters the unknown future, holding, not the hand of God, but a manual of conduct. His moral victory—the adoption of his moral code—drifts deeper and deeper into his past and becomes a memory to be honored. And that memory puts his present and his future under ironclad duress.

Even members of Alcoholics Anonymous, or most of them at least, know the folly of trying to predetermine their conduct for the rest of their life. So they live one day at a time, practicing on that day the total abstinence from alcohol that their vulnerability requires.

The Christian, too, borrows trouble if he tries today to chart his conduct through all of the tomorrows that face him. He may have his principles, I think he should, and they may be absolute. He may believe that his principles are universal—if anywhere, then everywhere—and that they are applicable to all human situations—if everywhere, then anywhere. But he should be cautious about saying that the laws by which he lives his life are eternal—if now, then always. "Always" is a province over which he has no control and the eternal belongs exclusively to God.

The fifth reason for rejecting legalism as authentic morality leads directly to the sixth. Legalism precludes the working of the Holy Spirit. In Paul's phrase, it "quenches the Spirit." Before Moses died, he gave his people two tablets—permanent, unchanging, absolute—by which all moral decisions were to be forever measured. In his death and resurrection Jesus Christ gave us a living spirit to accompany us in all life's long and circuitous pilgrimage—not something dead, anchored in the past, but something living and traveling with us into the future. We can choose the Decalogue as our sole guide and reject the Holy Spirit; or, we can accept the comforts of the Holy Spirit and let him be our counselor in all things, including the Decalogue. For his guide, the legalist looks to a finished event in the wilderness of Sinai; for his, the Christian looks to a continuing event which began when, in an upper room, the disciples of Christ "were all filled with the Holy Spirit." The God of the legalist, then, recedes into the past; the God of the Christian is always contemporary.

The approach to morality that I have been denouncing as vigorously as I can was demolished much more effectively by the apostle Paul. His letter to the Galatians, for example, is throughout a manifesto of Christian freedom from the law. Almost at random in this letter you can pick up verses that denounce legalism. Take verses 15-16 of the second chapter: "We ourselves, who are Jews by birth and not Gentile sinners, yet who know that a man is not justified by works of the law but through faith in Jesus Christ, even we have believed in Christ Jesus, in order to be justified by faith in Christ, and not by works of the law, because by works of the law shall no one be justified." Paul did not believe that the law is wholly without purpose and usefulness, nor did he equate freedom in Christ with moral anarchy. He knew the danger of giving to immature men the mature gospel of freedom from the law. But the risk had to be taken, for that Christ who supersedes the law had come.

The Extremities of Current Morality—Relativism

Now we turn from one pole of current morality to an exactly opposite one. But the swing is not from legalism to libertinism, nor is it from morality to immorality. Rather, we now take up another form of morality. The opposite of legalism is relativism, which is also known as contextualism, situational ethics, and the new morality. It could be said that the new morality is the current rebellion against legalism and against that thick stream of Puritanism that runs through so much of American Protestantism. It can be said at the outset that this approach to morality has much to commend it to the Christian conscience and imagination. The new morality claims the highest ethical insight as its warranty, and it therefore deserves our understanding, whether we want to give it our unreserved commitment or not.

The new morality holds that the test of love—the agape test—has to be applied to each isolated event of life extemporaneously as the sole criterion of good and bad. If conduct meets the test of love, it is good; if not, it is bad. Thus all laws, rules, commandments, and codes are disqualified. One thing alone—what love demands of the moment and what the moment demands of love—determines the rightness or wrongness of human conduct. Thus right and wrong are determined by the situation, by the context, and not by some eternal and absolute law. By this philosophy of morality nothing can be decided in advance, no moral rules can be prepared for life's expected or surprising events. No laws that we have been taught from our youth up—so this view says—are absolutely binding under all possible circumstances.

Indeed, say the new moralists, it is possible that under certain circumstances the love we have learned in Jesus Christ may demand that we lie, steal, kill, commit adultery. These circumstances may be rare; they may never occur; but, say the new moralists, they can occur. For by this theory there are no absolutes—no eternal, universal, changeless moral imperatives which might not somewhere at some time have to bow to the superior demands of love. The Christian therefore needs only to steep himself in the love of God as it is known in Jesus Christ and then enter each life situation confident that he will find there all the instructions he needs to act according to God's will.

If it seems that I am overstating what may be to some of you the shocking aspects of the new morality, then we should let one of the situationists speak for himself: Joseph Fletcher, professor of social ethics at the Episcopal Theological School, Cambridge, Massachusetts. Fletcher's views of the new morality theory are representative and he can be considered a spokesman for the situationists. In his latest book, *Moral Responsibility* (Westminster Press), Fletcher writes: "Hence in such a Christian ethic nothing has any worth except as it helps or hurts persons, either human or divine—God or neighbor or self . . . anything else, no matter what it is may be good or evil, right or wrong, according to the situation." Fletcher makes it plain that his "anything" includes theft, lying, fornication, and murder. All of these can be not merely necessary evils but positive goods. He gags a bit when he comes to such things as rape, incest, and cruelty to little children. But even here he must leave open the possibility that these normally vile human relations may in some situations be positively good.

Fletcher's categorical oversimplification of the Christian ethic has the appeal of simplicity. There is in its appeal to love a powerful attraction. But it is slippery ground and most people who try to stand on it plunge into the wholly unprincipled libertinism Fletcher disavows. Since I do not attempt here an analysis of Fletcher's view, I must take time to point out only two of the weaknesses in his system. First, he has a sub-Christian definition of love. He says: "Pinned down to its precise meaning, Christian love is 'benevolence,' literally, *Good will.*"

We would agree that benevolence is an aspect of Christian love, but merely an aspect and not the whole of it. Even if he is right in saying that good and evil are determined by what love demands in the situation, Fletcher is wrong in reducing love to goodwill, to benevolence, and in making *that* the determinant of right and wrong in a given situation. Next, he errs in assuming that he or anyone else is capable in any situation of deciding who shall be the beneficiary of benevolence. He says in one of his illustrations that Christian love would demand that the hospital's last unit of plasma be given to a young mother of three rather than to an old skidrow drunk. Why? Our sentiments are with the young mother, of course; but sentimental attachment is not necessarily Christian love. And, who makes us God in such a situation? Confronted by such dilemmas we do the best we can; and, perhaps we save the mother rather than the drunk. But it is not in that case *good* to condemn the drunk to death by helping the mother. Fletcher ignores the ambiguities of life; he ignores the fact that in many life situations we cannot do good without doing evil.

Fletcher prefers the harlot to the men who use her. He says: "Therefore in a familiar phrase, the prostitute is far more sinned against than sinning. She is infinitely closer to righteousness than are her customers." It is amusing to read such categorical statements from one who says that we must analyze the situation before passing judgment on who is right and who is wrong. In most cases the prostitute and her consorts are equally guilty. Both commercialize the other; both use the other as a "thing." And in some cases the prostitute is more culpable than her customers—for example, those campfollowers who, old and hardened in their profession, entice and debauch young men. What Jesus was saying in the story of the woman taken in adultery was not that the woman was innocent but that her guilt was shared by her accusers.

Also in this book there is an implied acceptance of the *Tea and Sympathy* theme, although Fletcher does not, as I recall, refer specifically to this play. In this play an older woman, supposedly in an act of benevolence, commits adultery with a young man to prove to him that he is not homosexual. This play blithely ignores the psychological fact that one heterosexual act tells us little about the potential homosexuality of its participants. It ignores the fact that the sexual act between an older married woman and a youth could have plunged him into disastrous conclusions about his own sexuality.

New moralists who use this play as proof that adultery can be a good deed, if benevolent, ignore the probability that the woman's motive was not unmixed benevolence, that she subverted the sexual act to a doubtful means, and that she was not acting benevolently toward that spouse to whom she had sworn fidelity. It would be much better for everyone concerned if young ministers would stop dragging *Tea and Sympathy* into their sermons and stick with the story of the woman taken in adultery, including all that it says about her, about her accusers, and about Jesus Christ. This story may or may not belong in the canon—scholars are in disagreement about this. But certainly *Tea and Sympathy* does not belong in the canon of Christian literature, nor does any document that exalts adultery to the level of redemption.

We shall turn soon to a proposed definition of authentic morality, but I must state first why the new morality—despite the commendations it deserves—must be repudiated on Christian grounds. There are at least four reasons why this doctrinaire, simplistic definition of Christian ethics will not do.

First, it is suspect in its origins. It has its current support in varying degrees of intensity in the writings of Joseph Fletcher; Bishop John A. T. Robinson, of *Honest to God* fame; Professor Paul Lehmann of Union Theological Seminary; and in the social theories and actions of many ministers for whom such churchmen and scholars are the final word. But Dr. Paul Ramsey, with whom I am at this point in agreement, finds the fountainhead of the new morality elsewhere.

In a book called *Deeds and Rules in Christian Ethics* (Scribner 1967), Ramsey writes: "The model for this freedom-in-love and an ethic of atomistic acts in Christian clothing is actually Jean Jacques Rousseau (making allowance for a liberal addition of Freudianism). For Rousseau there can be no bond (but only bargains) between two contracting individuals because there can and should be no bond established between one atomistic moment of will or consent and the next, and the next after that, which does not too much bind the latter and derogate upon the freedom of these later moments of willing."

If Ramsey is correct, as I think he is, then the fathers of contextual ethics are not Jesus Christ, with his love commandments; or Augustine, with his "Love God and do as you please"; or, in his own day, Dietrich Bonhoeffer.

Before I became the beneficiary of Ramsey's thoughts in this connection, I took up in a *Christian Century* editorial the question of moral nihilism in the United States and in this editorial wrote:

Something in the air has anesthetized the nerve of self-control, released the inner restraint, freed men of vital checks and balances. We are becoming the "anything goes" generation. Nearly 20 years ago in his *Values for Survival* Lewis Mumford indicted the moral nihilism which now rides triumphant over all other isms in American culture. He wrote: "For the last two hundred years a long succession of thinkers, from Diderot and Rousseau onward, have urged man to throw off his ancient taboos: to act on his impulses, yield to his desires, abandon measure in his gratifications." He was correct in his warning that the sweet voices of relaxation lure us toward disaster, correct in reminding us that man is neither wholly rational nor wholly good, correct in his insistence that in man there is a demonic nature which man must keep in chains. At the very time when man has more powers to control than he has ever had in his long history he is most reluctant to control himself. This combination can produce only catastrophe. Indeed, as Henry Adams predicted 60 years ago, the time when "explosives would reach cosmic violence" was matched precisely by the time when law disappeared "as theory or a priori principle." We made the bomb and, unrestrained by law or conscience, we dropped it. Was it on that August day when we first dropped the bomb that we declared ourselves forever free of all prohibitions? Or was the permissive mood antecedent to the dropping of the bomb? Never mind. The mood is with us, in us, a mood which scoffs at moral boundaries, ridicules rules, razes landmarks man's soul has looked to in ages past. Prohibitions, we have concluded, are evil per se. Since they restrain man they must necessarily be bad. Granted that prohibitions man imposes on man are just as likely to be evil as the permissions he grants himself, do we therefore conclude that even God cannot say No to man? Are we nearer to the truth when we taper and twist his "Thou shalt not" into a "Perhaps it would be better if you didn't"? Does Eden lie in that direction? "Love God," said Augustine, "and do as you please." Ah, yes. This is the law and the prophets. But since we do not love God, nothing is more pernicious than doing as we please. Permissiveness stands us on the edge of that precipitous descent down which man has repeatedly fallen from spiritual autocracy to anarchy to tyranny. It is a god which promises an utter, blissful freedom while delivering man to the ancient slaveries.

I am not suggesting that the new morality is responsible for the mood of libertinism that suffuses our culture. I do say that it encourages that mood, that it provides for it an air of religious sanction, and that its authority is the same authority appealed to by permissiveness. As Ramsey said, the freedom-in-love theory uses a Christian language, "but for all that, the basic philosophy of act-agapism is drawn from no Christian source." Some months ago my wife, our sixteen-year-old son, Thomas, and I were watching on television a documentary film on this generation's preoccupation with and pursuit of pleasure. As the more lurid images passed before our eyes, my wife said: "As sure as we are living, we are going the way of ancient Rome." To which Thomas replied, "Yes, we must beware of any presidential candidate who plays a fiddle. This is no time to have a Nero in the White House."

If the new morality is suspect first because of its parentage, it should be viewed cautiously, second, because of its products. In his little book *Christian Morals Today,* Bishop John A. T. Robinson states: "The trouble is that the traditional deductive morality [legalism] appears to be *anti-humanist.* I am sure it is not necessarily so, but this is how it looks." We can criticize the new morality in the same spirit and by the same measurement.

The trouble with relativism is that in its preoccupation with people it appears to be wholly unprincipled and therefore entirely permissive. I am sure that it is not necessarily so, but this is how it looks. You can get away with any kind of behavior you wish if your definitions and standards can call that behavior love. Whether situational ethics is authentic or not, whether or not this is the way men should "do" Christian truth, this view of Christian ethics is so easily distorted into license for immorality—especially into sexual permissiveness—that its popularity with broad segments of the high school and college age generation is easily understood. This does not mean, of course, that this simple view of Christian behavior can be judged, condemned, and repudiated because of its vulnerability to distortion.

Legalist codes of morality—it has been plentifully demonstrated—can be as readily abused as an ethic which professes no code. But if legalism has to be rebuked because of the way it looks and because of the excesses into which it degenerates, the new morality must be subjected to the same test. Legalism fails this test and so does the new morality. Indeed, the love-and-do-as-you-please ethic lends itself to translations and distortions that are more subtle, more facile in making evil appear good than is outright moral disobedience. If—as the relativists see it—nothing is always and everywhere wrong or eternally and universally right, if each situation has to be analyzed instantly and on the spot to see what it demands of love and what love demands of it, then all ethical problems must be entrusted to personal, individual, subjective, and spontaneous solutions. It is highly doubtful that man—even if he has "come of age"—is capable of handling such a challenge, of acting ethically in a situation to which he carries no previously structured ethical rules, or of "doing the truth" in a context in which he has the guidance only of his immediate judgment of what is loving in that context. To ask young people to make that kind of decision without the benefit of prohibitive and imperative norms betrays them and leaves them at the mercy of passions easily interpreted as love.

Third, the new morality clashes sharply with the realities of the human situation in that it views each act of life as separate from all other acts, each moment as disconnected from each other moment, each person as independent from all other persons and spontaneous love—benevolence to the immediately confronted person—as the only norm that can be applied to each act, each moment, and each person. Thus law, tradition and all revelation, except love, are annulled, and spontaneous love remains not only the ultimate but also the exclusive test of the rightness or wrongness of human action in a given situation. If the moment when the ethical decision must be made stands in imperial isolation from the past—that is, from law, tradition, experience, and revelation prior to the moment—and from the future—that is, from its consequences—then we have learned in all Christian experience nothing that can give us ethical insight and instruction today and nothing to communicate to tomorrow. But this is not the case.

The new morality—contextual morality—is in fact defective by its own definition. It fails to take into consideration the total human situation. When one person or two or more are confronted with the need for a moral decision, they, their need, their mood, seldom make up the total situation. The past is always there with bonds and pledges made in love to other individuals and groups, with the lessons that have been learned and the insights that previous experiences have produced. The future is there in the trusts other people have invested in the persons involved in the particular situation, in the consequences which will result from the decisions made in the situation. And the present, the supreme concern of the new moralists, includes people who at the moment are not on the scene physically.

Every act of adultery includes not two people but at least three. At least one betrayed spouse is present and at times two. Every false witness involves the liar, the one presumably helped by the lie, and the one wounded by the lie. Every theft deprives not only the individual who is robbed, and who if wealthy may not be greatly hurt by the theft, but also the whole social fabric. There are no isolated human experiences in which one person or more can decide with references only to themselves what is good behavior and what is not. And God is always a part of the context, always present with a will, judgment, and love wider than the bare and immediate human scene, more enduring than the fleeting moment.

The new morality, the completely ruleless and unstructured morality, boasts that it has relinquished all authority to the love we know in Christ. But in practice it does not do so. On the contrary it trusts everything to the dominant impulse of the moment, and that impulse may be wholly foreign to the Christian love that has its focus on the sacredness of persons and the holiness of community. The new morality, moreover, authorizes the individual to make final, crucial decisions solely on the basis of his personal appraisal of the situation and with no reference to life-giving rules—and often at a time when he is least competent to make such decisions.

I know a clergyman, a devotee of situation ethics, who says that he has to decide every morning whether to fornicate or not to fornicate. Most of us are not under the burden of having to make that decision day after day. In love for our spouses and for that person whom we do not want to treat as a "thing," in love for ourselves and for the kind of person we want to be, in love for the gospel and for its plain prohibition of fornication, we have decided against this kind of human relation. It does not occur to us that we shall do otherwise, and we do not have to remind ourselves day after day that we have said our no to the kind of life that would degrade us, betray those who trust us, and make an instrument of pleasure out of some other human being. We made this decision when we could think clearly, when our thoughts were not warped by our passions. The decision was made not in automatic surrender to some external law but in loving concern for ourselves and for other people. We do not boast of this commitment, for we know that man is a sinful creature and that he is most liable to sin at the point of his proudest virtue. We take this commitment with us into every situation, not as a conscious thought, but as a disposition. And we thus reduce the temptation produced by any situation, for temptation without always implies desire within. We have prayed that we shall not be led into temptation and we have tamed that desire that makes us vulnerable to temptation.

We have for the same loving reasons made commitments against theft, false witness, murder, the abuse of children and animals. These commitments have not been specified in detail. They are the expressions—sometimes conscious, sometimes not—of our commitment to Christ. These decisions evolve from our decision to live the Christian life. If we fail—as in one of these categories or another we shall—we will not pass off our failure as in reality a good deed. We will know that we have failed, that we have sinned against ourselves, our neighbor, and our God. We will pray for and receive forgiveness and we will begin anew. There will be decisions that will have to be made on the spur of the moment, in the heat of a situation in which we are taken by surprise. But even then we can draw strength from prior commitments.

In making their decision that temptations have to be resolved in the midst of the situation and solely on the basis of love, the new moralists have obviously paid little or no attention to what we are taught in the biblical story of the temptations of Jesus. In each of three instances Jesus banished the tempter, not by asking what his situation demanded of love, but by quoting Scripture verses. This does not mean that Jesus used the Scriptures as a talisman, as a magic wand to wave in the face of the devil. Rather, it means that in this battle he refused to be cut off from his spiritual resources. He refused to fight this crucial battle bereft of those weapons he had acquired prior to the battle. He had decisions to make but he made them on the basis of decisions already made.

This story is the classical New Testament illustration of the handling of temptation. The classical Old Testament illustration is the story of Joseph and Potiphar's wife. When young Joseph was tempted by Potiphar's wife, he did not toy with the idea that this woman might need him to restore her wholeness and that his lying with her might be benevolent and redemptive. No, he did four things. He remembered his obligation to his master, he recalled the trust bestowed on him, he called the wicked suggestion a sin against God, and he fled the woman's presence. I commend these two stories to the study of the new moralists.

So we can now summarize the deficiencies of these two extremities of current morality in the following way. Legalism tends to make men servile; relativism tends to make men libertine. Legalism makes a shrine out of an event in the past; the new morality hallows a fleeting instant in the present. Legalism externalizes and mechanizes morality; relativism internalizes and subjectivizes morality. Legalism writes hard contracts between men; the new morality cancels all bonds between men, except those directly related to the immediate situation. Legalism precludes the counsel of the Holy Spirit; contextual ethics substitutes the will and mood of man for the counsel of the Holy Spirit. Legalism encourages immorality by its rigidity; the new morality encourages immorality by its imprecision. Legalism tends to ignore man; relativism exalts man as the ultimate arbiter of good and evil.

2
Authentic Morality Defined

Genuine Christian morality combines aspects of legalism and relativism so subtly that what results is radically different from either. It is rooted in Matthew 22:37-40. Asked about the good life, Jesus replied: "You shall love the Lord your God with all your heart, and with all your soul, and with all your mind. This is the great and first commandment. And a second is like it. You shall love your neighbor as yourself. On these two commandments depend all the law and the prophets." Several facts stick out in this Scripture passage.

First, however proper it is in our time to accent the humanistic aspect of the gospel, Jesus in this reference gives priority—however slight—to another kind of love, man's love for God. There are actually three commands here, two of them stated and one implied: love God, love neighbor, love self. Second, both love and law appear in Jesus' description of the good life—not one or the other but both. Third, the dominant theme in these commandments is clearly love rather than law. So we must conclude with the new moralists that love is the dominant authority ruling the true Christian's behavior, the sole criterion of what is good and what is bad.

Love is central and the law is peripheral; love is primary and the law is secondary. Live perfectly by the law, wholly by the prophets, but if you do not live in love, you do not know the good life. Yet in Jesus' description of the good life there is provision for rules, for a structured morality based on love, for disciplines through which the good life becomes actual and authentic: "On these two commandments depend all the law and the prophets." Neither of the extreme forms of morality, then, is in itself and exclusive of the other an authentic morality; for the Christian life must in some way incorporate, as Christ's commandments do, both love and law.

Love is not an amorphous, unstructured sentiment; not a combination of warmth and helplessness; not an indefinable passion, an uncontrollable impulse, nor emotional glow. On the contrary—as we shall see—the depths and heights and breadths of Christian love are such that it must be defined, expounded, explored, learned, and absorbed far in advance of the life situations which demand it. And for this reason it has to be broken open to us so that we grasp its fulness by seeing the dependent parts into which it falls.

The maxims and illustrations in the Sermon on the Mount have merit for us solely because they unfold specifically the love that came to us in Jesus Christ. But without the commandments and teachings of the Sermon on the Mount, the love Christ commanded men to have for God and men would be vague and sentimental. The apostle Paul was magnificent when, in 1 Corinthians 13, he praised love as "the greatest of these," but he was equally helpful when, in Romans 12, he told us how love behaves in the world.

Let us consider, then, the five dimensions of authentic morality, developing a definiton that will enable us to ask with some confidence what effect the media of mass communication have on character and personality. We define authentic morality by looking at its five dimensions: its focus, its objective, its habitat, its criterion, and its source. And we must ask as we do so whether each of these dimensions has its origin in the Christian faith.

The Focus: People

The focus of authentic morality is people. There are pseudomoral systems in which the concentration centers on things other than people: institutions, abstract principles, tradition, the state, law and order, culture, property, religious revelation and teaching, the church. But the primary concern of genuine Christian morality is people. This morality is interested in other things—custom, history, theology, social structure—only in relation to their effect on people.

Authentic morality asks about a business, not whether it has profits or losses or a good rating with Dun and Bradstreet, but what its effect is on its employees and its customers. Although it provides needful goods and services and its records appear well in the black in its annual financial reports, it may be oppressing its employees and deceiving its customers. In that case it is immoral.

Authentic morality asks about a school system, not whether its curriculum and its equipment are the latest and the best, but what the system does to the students. It asks about a government, not whether it is politically and militarily strong or weak, but what its total effect is on the governed. It asks about programs of community organization and development, not whether they get things done, but whether in the process of getting things done they help or harm people.

Genuine morality does not focus on creeds or laws, doctrines or theories, classes and colors, but on people. It assumes that people have primary importance over everything else in God's creation. This view is sometimes dismissed by some Christians as humanism. It is humanism; but it should not be dismissed, for humanism can be Christian and Christianity should be humanistic. That is, Christianity should focus on people. Humanism has many roots and some of those roots reach deep into the Bible. Although some parts of the Old Testament are saturated with legalism and some parts exalt sites, monuments, and rites above man, there are passages substantiating the idea that the person has an autonomous value superior to all other values. Jesus cited the most convincing of these passages.

When Jesus and his disciples were walking through the grain field on the sabbath and he, to their astonishment, plucked grain, he said to them: "Have you not read what David did, when he was hungry, and those who were with him: how he entered the house of God and ate the bread of the Presence, which it was not lawful for him to eat nor for those who were with him, but only for the priests?" (Matt. 12:3-4). Jesus used this historical incident to show that human need has priority over the house of God, sacred objects, and revered professions. And the actions and teachings of Jesus himself are replete with the insistence that man has priority over all things secular and sacred. There are three principal foci in the New Testament: God, man, and their confrontation in Jesus Christ.

Everything else is secondary—rites, institutions, sites, religious orders, and laws. Christianity is God-centered, man-centered, Christ-centered.

Perhaps this point might become more acceptable to us if we substituted another term for humanism. But there is no good reason why we should not redeem the term from those political or social connotations repugnant to us and why we should not in the future speak positively of Christian humanism. Whether we accept the term or not, as Christians we must accept the concept, for the whole of the New Testament focuses on all sorts and conditions of men—not on sacred stones, sacred streams, and sacred sites but on people. We can call this heavy accent on the priority of people what we will—humanist, personalist, or Christian—but we must not ignore and dismiss it. If we do, we at once cut the nerve of Christian morality, for that morality as it appears in the New Testament focuses on people.

Unfortunately, the Christian churches have often made the mistake of concentrating their interest on something other than people: abstract theologies and doctrines; church buildings and ecclesiastical differences; and petty theological disputes. Indeed, white people or influential people rather than on people; numbers of people rather than on people themselves; prestige; superficial ecclesiastical differences; and petty theological disputes. Indeed, in most cases in which the churches have gone wrong they have done so primarily because they permitted people to drift or thrust them from the center of their concern. When the churches ceased to be humanistic, ceased to focus on people, they ceased to be Christian and ceased to be moral.

In the churches today there is a long overdue but most gratifying development—an awakening awareness of the priority of people. In the past you would have expected to find this acknowledgment of the sacredness of man in those churches associated with the social gospel. But now you find this accent also in churches that until most recently condemned the social gospel.

For example, I discovered in an editorial in the June, 1967, issue of *Decision*—the magazine published by The Billy Graham Evangelistic Association and edited by Sherwood Wirt—some statements that could have been written by Harry Emerson Fosdick or Walter Rauschenbusch. These statements would have been denounced by conservative evangelicals a decade ago as modernistic, probably even as communistic. This editorial made the following declarations: "Jesus was deliberately placing humanity, the life of man, above all social and religious considerations. He was esteeming man, Homo sapiens, as the purpose for which the state and its social institutions existed. The sabbath was only the means; man was the end. . . . On the basis of a survey of Scripture, it can be said that the case for a Christian social conscience built around Jesus' concern for the total welfare of men has an excellent base of support." So, even the conservative evangelicals are beginning to see that the focus of the gospel is total man in his total situation.

Some of this new emphasis on the centrality of man is due to the perils of our time, and some to our deeper understanding of the meaning of the gospel. Some of it has its source in Christian thinkers of our time, and some of it—much of it indeed—comes from our non-Christian environment. We should not be jealous or resentful of this influence but grateful for it, thankful that God has used people whom we might dismiss as "children of darkness" to open the eyes of the "children of light."

I am thinking of atheistic humanists and angry young men who through art, drama, and literature rebuke the indifference of Christians for people. I am thinking of Albert Camus who, in his book *The Myth of Sisyphus,* and other writings, exalted the dignity and the reconciliation of man "without the aid of eternal values." I am thinking of Martin Buber who in his *I and Thou* enriched our understanding of human communion; of Erich Fromm to whom, I believe, we are indebted for the phrase, "Man is not a thing." Men like Bertrand Russell, Jean-Paul Sartre, and Julian Huxley would spurn the supernatural aspects of our faith; yet, they would insist that man is the measure of things. Thus, unintentionally of course, these men have helped drive us back to what we know was the view of man incarnated in Jesus Christ. We are indebted to any man who, whether he is one of us or not, draws our wandering concern and our vacillating behavior back to the truth of our faith.

In a little article on Bunyan's *The Pilgrim's Progress* in the August

13, 1966, issue of the *Saturday Review,* Kenneth Rexroth reminded us of those nonspiritual but ethical people who believe that salvation—if there is such a thing—"comes through the assumption of unlimited liability, person for person." Surely there is much more to the good life than these people have discovered. But the question for us is whether they know and serve something essential to the good life and yet foreign to us.

I suggest therefore that the first test to be applied when later we ask about the effect of a particular medium of communication on morality is a test of ourselves. Are we really concerned about the effect of that medium on people or are we concerned about its effect on things secondary to people? Does our deepest focus fall on the national image, static customs, honored institutions, memories of how much better things and people were in the old days, organized religion, our personal fear of painful change, or on people? The media of mass communication—we shall note later—are causing massive, deep changes in the patterns of American life. Are we anxious about these patterns themselves, or, are we really concerned about the effect of old patterns and new patterns on the quality of American life? Let us not deceive ourselves.

Manufacturers and sellers of buggies at the turn of this century had a difficult time viewing the automobile as anything other than a monstrous invention of the devil that would do the people incalculable mischief. In moralistically condemning the automobile—as some of them did—they probably believed sincerely that they were championing the best interests of the people. (Considering what the automobile has done to us, perhaps they were right.) They were in fact trying to defend their own interests.

What are our motives as we question the effect of mass media on morality? Does our code of morality have this first and indispensable dimension? Does it focus on people?

The Objective: Persons

If authentic morality focuses on people, what is its objective in doing so? What is the purpose of morality? We must not assume that there is an obvious and universally acceptable answer to that question. In the minds of a great many people the sole purpose of morality is to maintain the status quo. Morality for them is a legitimately defensive instrument by which institutions, customs, and traditions beneficial to them are preserved. For example, there are Old Testament scholars who say that the Ten Commandments were not delivered to man by God but were invented by men to protect and preserve a patriarchal society. The patriarchs, being outnumbered, they say, had to develop a moral system that would safeguard their possessions. And, in order to enforce it, they attributed the system to God's authorship.

The second of the two tablets of commandments does look like a manifesto for property rights. If the patriarchs could impose this code on their people, then they would defend themselves against their numerous and potentially rebellious children. They would defend their lives against murder; their many, sometimes restless, wives against adulterous lovers; their material property against thieves and covetous eyes; their reputation against slander.

Whether or not this theory explains the origin of the Decalogue, the law has many times been cited against oppressed peoples who have threatened to rise up and overthrow their oppressors.

But we have a much better, more reliable illustration of the use of moral codes to maintain an oppressive social order. In *The Racial Problem in Christian Perspective,* published by Harper and Brothers in 1959, I told the story of Charles Cotesworthy Pinckney, who, in 1829, suggested to the Agricultural Society of South Carolina that religion should be taught to Negro slaves to make them docile, obedient, and industrious. Pinckney wanted to make them moral—after a fashion—to prevent "reluctance to labor," "feigned sickness," and "theft, falsehood, and many other vices." What Pinckney did openly in slavery in attempting to tame Negroes with religion, we have to this day continued to do to the Negro in the United States, but with more subtlety. To the white man "a good Negro" is one who has accepted the weak, passive virtues that hamper his rebellion against the white man's oppressive system. And "a bad Negro" is to the white man one who defies codes of legality, gentility, and morality that stand between him and his realization of himself as a full man. The use of morality as a defender of unjust social systems is a perversion of morality.

Second, it is not the purpose of authentic morality to make people good. Consider some of the synonyms of the word "good": kind, friendly, well-behaved, agreeable, pleasant, proper, virtuous, pious, devout. None of these is the aim of authentic morality. Jesus Christ did not die for us so that we might faithfully recite the Boy Scout Law. He did not come, someone has said, to make bad men good; he came to make dead men live. This is his avowed purpose as expressed in John 10:10: "The thief comes only to steal and kill and destroy; I came that they may have life, and have it abundantly." The word "abundantly" in this text has a qualitative as well as a quantitative significance. It refers to time but even more to intensity, to chronology but especially to character, to length but particularly to fulness.

We can say, then, that the objective of authentic morality is to focus on people in such a way as to transform them into persons. We can say that the purpose of true morality is to produce personality, even though the word "personality" in popular use means winsomeness. For in its neglected use the word means, according to *Webster's New Collegiate Dictionary,* quality or state of being personal, or of being a person; personal existence or identity. Some people, using other terms, would prefer to say that the aim of morality is to enable man to be man—not a thing, or an animal, or a machine. And still others would say that morality's aim is to make it possible for human beings to be human.

Man has a yet unexplored range of mental and emotional and communal capabilities. Authentic morality acts within him and on him to push these capabilities toward their ultimate capacity. There is a difference—in most cases a laudatory one—between man and the other members of the animal kingdom. Genuine morality operates within man and between men to widen this difference. Man is a part of nature, yet he has transcended and established his dominion over nature. True morality extends and dignifies this dominion. Rabbi Abraham J. Heschel has said: "Perhaps the most amazing aspect about man is what is latent in him." The purpose of authentic morality is to make possible and visible in man the glory that is hidden.

The full man, the real person, has integrity, wholeness. The tensions and conflicts between his several selves are resolved. He is not at war with himself. His name, unlike that of the blind man who cried out at Jesus, is not Legion. It was once said of Albert Einstein, "Einstein is all of a piece. There is no division in him." That may not have described Einstein; it does describe true man. And the end of real morality is to increase the number of people about whom that can be truly said.

The integrity of the full man includes an integration of his life with the lives of all men. He is at peace with them as he is at peace with himself. His internal oneness overflows into an external oneness. Authentic morality is the glue of that oneness. The full man, the real person, has an integrity that relates him to himself, to other men, and to God, the Other—"the Beyond that is within." This, indeed, is what salvation means in strictest terms of Christian theology and in New Testament concepts. It means the elimination of brokenness, the restoration of wholeness at all levels of man's being and in all his relationships. Authentic morality focuses on people with the aim of producing such wholeness.

Therefore we can conclude that whatever helps produce and sustain true man, real persons, is moral. Whatever destroys persons or prevents the development of persons is immoral. There is no other morality; there is no other immorality. It is immoral to allow people to starve in a world in which there is abundant food, not only because unnecessary starvation is cruel to their bodies, but even more because malnutrition deprives men of their opportunity to be real persons.

War is immoral, not only because it breaks a commandment against killing, but even more because all wars—just or unjust—bestialize all men who are caught up in their evil webs.

Religious bigotry and racial prejudice and their products—segregation and exploitation—are doubly immoral because the bigoted and the prejudiced break their oneness with all men and by oppressive acts make it difficult for those whom they despise to be real persons. Again, the white man's greatest sin against the Negro is not that he has denied him the right to have and to belong—evil as these denials are—but that in doing so the white man has denied the Negro the right to be.

The habitual use of narcotics and the luring of other people into such addictions is immoral, not only because narcotics harm the body, but primarily because they destroy the man. Whatever keeps people from being persons is immoral.

In his book *The Christian Life* (The Covenant Life Curriculum Press), Waldo Beach stresses the inwardness of morality in the following word: "Insofar as the formulation of Christian ethics is in harmony with the mind of Christ it transcends *any* legalism of 'doing' in the name of an ethic of grace, of inner 'being.'" Although normally morality relates to "doing," to acts committed between people, Beach is quite correct in saying that in essence morality is a question of being, the being of the one who acts or whose attitude could be translated into action and the being of the one toward whom the act or attitude is directed.

It was the intention of Jesus to make this accent on being unmistakably clear when in the Sermon on the Mount he said to his disciples: "You have heard that it was said, 'You shall not commit adultery.' But I say to you that every one who looks at a woman lustfully has already committed adultery with her in his heart" (Matt. 5:27-28). The act of adultery is nevertheless worse than the thought. For the thought debases one being and the act debases two. But the damage in each case is far more internal than external.

The primary ethical question is not "What do we obey?"—legalism—or, "How do we behave?"—moralism—or, "What do we want?" —libertinism—but, "Who are we?" Let me fortify this point by quoting two respected theologians who come at this issue from different theological premises, Rufus Jones and Paul Tillich. Rufus Jones, the Quaker mystic, said:

Conscience, as we have seen, in its loftiest stage, is no longer negative. It affirms a unique personal life. It has a positive aspect; it is the knowledge of a higher will than that of our momentary, isolated self. *It is the voice of our ideal self, our complete self, our real self, laying its call upon the will.* This voice, this call, comes up out of the deep, for the ideal which a man has and by which he shapes his life is, as I have said, subconscious rather than explicit and thought out. But it is not something foreign to the man himself, it is not something external to him, it is not some one particular instinct among other instincts. It is the complete self voicing its ideals and exerting its sway over passion and impulse and momentary self and courses of action which fall below our vision.[1]

In language that is quite different, Paul Tillich came to essentially the same conclusions in his book *Morality and Beyond* (Harper and Row). Indeed, in Tillich's statement we find some of the mystical tone associated with Quakers like Jones. Tillich said, "For us the 'Will of God' is manifest in our essential being; and only because of this can we accept the moral imperative as valid. It is not a strange law that demands our obedience, but the 'silent voice' of our own nature as man, and as man with an individual character." And earlier in this book he had written: "The moral imperative is the command to become what one potentially is, a *person* within a community of persons."

Both of these theologians would agree that being a person in the midst of persons requires a life that allows and helps other men to be persons.

So the question that we should ask about the impact of the media of mass communication on our society is whether they help people become persons or prevent their being persons. Do they facilitate and promote man's emergence as true man—integrated, independent, and responsible—or do they transform man into a receptacle, a puppet, an echo?

Do modern forms of communication help man to be his full self? Do they discover and encourage the unfolding of his latent possibilities? Or, do they reduce all men to a stale pattern of conformity, blighting those individual traits that add charm and possibility to the whole society? Does mass communication inevitably mean the emergence of a mass mind, an intellectual ant heap, an amorphous religiosity, and a collective ethic? Will the media eventually standardize all human behavior at the level of the lowest conduct in the society, or will they enrich the general tone and character of the people? Will they help or hinder the production of persons in the midst of persons?

---

[1]Harry Emerson Fosdick (ed.), *Rufus Jones Speaks to Our Time* (New York: The Macmillan Co., 1951), p. 81. Used by permission.

The Habitat: Freedom

What are the conditions under which this kind of morality can flourish? What is its natural habitat? Let us begin our answer to this question with a statement first made—I believe—by Aristotle. This Greek philosopher said that a slave cannot be ethical because he has no will of his own. Aristotle assumed correctly that an act is neither ethical nor unethical unless it is wilful. When the slave is compelled to transfer his will to his master he can no longer be ethical.

It follows that to whatever degree man is overpowered by, or surrenders to, the coercions of external powers, to that extent he loses the ability to be moral. He becomes under these coercions not immoral but amoral. For example, famine, disease, and ignorance can become, as we have noted, such austere tyrants that they rob man of his volition and his aspirations. When a human being's whole caloric supply is expended day after day to keep his body alive there is little possibility that he will ever know his latent self or help any other man become a real person.

In the case of the alcoholic or the drug-addict, the tyrant is within rather than without; but the result is the same. As his addiction increases, the addict passes from the stage of immorality, in which he wilfully destroys himself, to the stage where his destroyed self is no longer capable of making effective decisions. It is an utter waste of time to rebuke an addict and to challenge him to buck up, get a grip on himself, and straighten out his life. He is a slave and cannot be ethical.

We must conclude therefore that the habitat of authentic morality is freedom. Only a free man can be a real person involved in the production of persons.

Some of the slaveries that rob us of our freedom and volition are much more subtle than those mentioned thus far. Religious legalism, as we have seen, can be a tyrant that substitutes its authority for our will. Legalism can make us good in the common sense of the word, but it cannot make us ethical. Indeed, as the apostle Paul would say, the more subservient we become to the law—the more it becomes our master and we its slave—the less our opportunity to be moral men. "Now before faith came," said Paul to the Galatians, "we were confined under the law, kept under restraint until faith should be revealed. So that the law was our custodian until Christ came, that we might be justified by faith. But now that faith has come, we are no longer under a custodian; for in Christ Jesus you are all sons of God, through faith."

Fear, like legalism, is a tyrant that can make us good but at the same time preclude our being moral. To this day many men who grew up in my day and in the generations before do not know whether they abstained from fornication because they were moral men or because they were afraid. Fear of pregnancy, of venereal disease, and of discovery were in those days powerful though certainly not infallible inhibitors of fornication. But the pill, penicillin, and the anonymity provided by our mobile society have changed all that. For the first time in his history man can make a purely moral decision about fornication. It can be said that these three new factors have, by reducing fear, enabled man to be unquestionably moral in a situation in which he could be immoral, prudential, or perhaps moral. Fear can produce cautious men but it cannot produce real persons.

At this point we must note that the effect of mass media on morality must be tested from several angles. We are interested, of course, in the moral quality of the material communicated by the media and the purpose of that communication. What ideas do the media broadcast over the country? How much direct propagandizing for these ideas do the media employ; and, especially in the case of advertising and entertainment, what mores do the media press upon the people by subtle persuasion?

We will take up these and similar questions. But we must also ask a somewhat different question. That is, do the media of mass communication enlarge the range of freedom in which man can be a free moral agent, fully and truly man, or do they restrict his freedom? We will not be able to make a summary judgment about mass communication as such, nor about any one of the media; for the effect of the whole field and of the particular media on man's freedom varies sharply and greatly from media to media, time to time, and place to place.

What we discover, then, will both please and displease us. But we shall be asking about media the kind of question Malcolm Cowley answered about literature in a July 7, 1962, article in the *Saturday Review*. In "Artists, Conscience, and Censors," Cowley said:

> Whether literature makes us better Christians, citizens, husbands, wives, or parents is a subject for debate. I suppose the realistic answer is that some books do and some don't. Some very great authors have been dangerous models to emulate in daily life. But if they were truly great, they performed one service for every reader by broadening his range of sympathies and his consciousness of what goes on around him—by making him see and hear and appreciate what he might otherwise have missed—while at the same time deepening his emotions. The great authors have made life seem richer, more interesting, and more worth the living than it would have seemed without their work. In a single phrase, they have helped to create the myths by which we live.

This is a high tribute to the impact of literature on man's freedom as a person. What shall we have to say when we subject the mass media to a similar test? Do they enlarge or restrict the freedom that is the habitat of authentic morality?

The Criterion: Love

We have already agreed with the new moralists that love is the only intrinsic good and that authentic morality is love-centered and love-empowered. Since this view is rooted in the spirit, teachings, and conduct of Jesus, it is—as Douglas Rhymes put it in the title of his book—no new morality. But the new moralists veer toward libertinism, because in giving love a shallow definition they fail to take into account its demand for structures, for laws, for certain absolutes in human behavior. It is therefore most important that we give the word "love" its highest, fullest definition when we acknowledge that it is the criterion of authentic morality.

In his latest book Joseph Fletcher says: "Pinned down to its precise meaning, Christian love is 'benevolence,' literally. *Good will.*" If we give to "benevolence" the full meaning Fletcher rightly insists the word should have, his is still a most inadequate definition. He offers us a part and insists that it is the whole.

We are much closer to the truth if we accept the definition by a Jewish secularist, Erich Fromm, and by a Christian theologian, Paul Tillich. I suspect that Fromm and Tillich came independently of each other to their common understanding of love. Fromm's *The Art of Loving* (Harper and Row)—it has nothing to do with the techniques of sexual love—is the best non-Christian definition of love I know. Fromm says that love is "union under the condition of preserving one's integrity. . . . In love the paradox occurs that two beings become one and yet remain two." Tillich explores this concept of love much more deeply in his brief work *Love, Power, and Justice* (Oxford University Press), and gives us a more precise definition. He says that love is the drive toward, the power enabling, and the consummation of unity.

In all of its forms—charitable, benevolent, sexual, filial, aesthetic—love is the desire for, the energy that produces, and the experience of oneness. It is this meaning of love that enables the Gospel of John to say that "God is love." For this is to say that God is the spirit who wills and empowers and is in himself the consummation of oneness. So, though we cannot say that God is compassion, benevolence, sexual attraction, family attachment—all forms of love—we can say that God is love. It is this meaning of love that emerges in Jesus' prayer for the church. The Gospel of John records his prayer: "That they may all be one; even as thou, Father, art in me, and I in thee, that they also may be in us." And it is this love to which Paul sings in the thirteenth chapter of 1 Corinthians—not merely goodwill but the often unaccepted oneness that all men have in the God who is one.

According to this definition, to love oneself means not to be selfish or vain but to desire wholeness, to be *a* person rather than many conflicting selves. To love the neighbor is not merely to wish him well, to have his interest at heart, to refuse to use him as an end, but is, even more, to see in him the separated self and to desire that by one of love's ties this separation will be ended. And to love God is to desire oneness with him who made us and in whom we "live and move and have our being."

Genuine love—the desire for, the power enabling, and the realization of oneness—is vulnerable to many distortions. Since the objective of love is unity rather than mere union, it is distorted wherever any kind of coercion is employed to achieve union rather than unity in the name of love. To a sick mind, rape may seem a form of love; but it forces one of the persons into an undesired physical and emotional relation. Rape is always and absolutely wrong, not only because it makes an instrument out of a person, but also because it profanes a physical expression of love.

Tyrannical and total domination of the mind and spirit of another person under the pretext of love may secure union but it cannot achieve unity. It is always and absolutely wrong for one person, by virtue of some physical control or coercive personality, to take captive the mind and spirit of some other person in the name of love. Parents often make this mistake with their children. By this route they possess their children, but they do not love them.

Moreover, genuine love honors a priority of relations. Incest dishonors an unbreakable physical relation in order to indulge one unnecessary in love's economy. It cannot be good, whatever the new moralists say to the contrary. Fornication squanders permanent unities with oneself and with other people—real and potential relations—on momentary ones. It may be pardonable, but it is not good.

Adultery, which the new moralists say can conceivably be redemptive, is on the contrary always destructive. It repudiates a primary relation to a spouse, to society, to God, and to self by engaging in a secondary relation that may or may not have any of the credentials of love. The mosaic of genuine love allows us to love some people in ways that we should not, and should not want to, love other people. One of our mistakes is that we construe one of love's parts as the whole. Compassion, charity, goodwill, filial affection, sexual attraction, patriotism—these are some of the parts of love, ways in which love properly secures its expression. But genuine love is not any one of these parts.

The German philosopher Max Scheler once said, "Every love is love for God taking a rest by the wayside." We can say that every love expresses in some specific way the mystery and the essence of that genuine love that wills all things to be one. Genuine love is permissive, imperative, and prohibitive. Its *no* is implicit in its *yes*.

Love transforms separation into oneness. There are distortions of love that seek to eliminate separation without transforming it into oneness. Psychologically, it can be said that alcoholism and drug-addiction are love gone wrong. They substitute personal oblivion for personal fragmentation. This was understood two thousand years ago when Christians were told not to be drunk with wine but to be filled with the spirit. They were advised to invite into themselves that Spirit that would provide them internal harmony and to avoid those spirits that would merely and momentarily deaden their awareness of the wars raging within them. Murder and false witness are the counterparts of addiction. Murder tries to end human separation by killing the body of the estranged; false witness does so by trying to destroy the character and reputation of the estranged. In each case the separation is intolerable, and the separate one rather than the separation is eliminated. Voluntary addiction to alcohol and to narcotics, murder, and false witness are always and absolutely wrong. They not only destroy or threaten to destroy persons but they also corrupt that love that is the measure of all human deeds.

So, we can say of certain human acts that they are always and absolutely immoral. Love has written its laws against these deeds. To be sure, these are not the only evils—in some cases not the worst—that love condemns. But they are representative of those evil deeds that men often ascribe to, and justify, as expressions of love. It is a naïve waste of time and perhaps an immoral one to speculate, as some men do, on the possibility that there perhaps may be bizarre situations in which these evils are not only necessary but positively good.

By condemning incest, fornication, adultery, murder, false witness, and voluntary addiction, we are neither writing a new Decalogue nor endorsing legalistic moral codes. Rather, we are saying that love—the only intrinsic good—has its derivatives, its laws. If we live in the love that wills oneness such conduct as we have described is for us no longer optional. To the immoral man, love has said its *no* so that to the real person, the true man, it may say its *yes*.

Since we have heard Tillich on love, we should also hear him on law. He understood love's demand for structures and codes. In

Morality and Beyond, he wrote: "Indeed, law and institutions are required. They are required by love itself. For every individual, even the most creative, needs given structures that embody the experience and wisdom of the past, that liberate him from the necessity of having to make innumerable decisions on his own, and that show him a meaningful way to act in most situations. . . . No system of ethics can ever become an actual power without laws and institutions . . . but love is always able to break through them in a new *kairos,* and to create new laws and new systems of ethics."

Tillich saw not only love's demand for laws but also human nature's need for structures. Barbara W. Tuchman, author of *The Guns of August,* put this point most ably in an address to the National Conference on higher education at a meeting in Chicago. She said: "Most people need a structure, not only to fall into but to fall out of. . . . It occurs to me that much of the student protest now may be a testing of authority, a search for that line to fall out of and when it isn't there they become angrier because they feel more lost, more abandoned than ever. . . . We seem to be afflicted by a widespread and eroding reluctance to take any stand on any values, moral, behavioral or esthetic." This is, I believe, a correct understanding of the human need for structures. We will do well to provide and endorse the structures human nature needs and love permits and demands.

The Source: God

Authentic morality focuses on people for the purpose of producing persons in a milieu of freedom, according to the standards imposed by genuine love. What, then, is the source of this morality? Is it the product of a natural evolutionary process, or is it the gift of God? Must we say of authentic morality, as we have defined it, that it is the best description of his potential self man-come-of-age has yet devised, or do we see in it a "givenness" that can come only from something beyond man? Is the authentic morality deductive or inductive? Does it start with God or with man? Is it a revelation or an achievement?

Christian legalists have an incorrect understanding of the essence and quality of morality but a correct understanding of its origin.

It is from God, through revelation by his Son, who is Lord, Saviour, and true man.

The new moralists excel the legalists in their definition of morality; but, with some exceptions, they incorrectly identify its source. Starting as they do with man, for them authentic morality tends to be man's discovery of himself rather than God's disclosure of his will for man. One of the differences between humanism per se and Christian humanism is that humanism focuses on man and begins with him; whereas, Christian humanism focuses on man but begins with God. The New Testament is the story of what God has done for and with man, not the story of what man has done in a search for himself and for God. It reveals God's acts, not man's achievement. Its accent falls heavy on God's grace and light on man's works. New Testament morality is deductive and inductive.

The disciples of situation ethics say that love, translated as benevolence, is the only absolute. There is an absolute other than benevolence, even Jesus Christ, true man and real person. In him we see what God wills for man, what he wants each of his children to be in the full realization of himself. The man Christ Jesus is the absolute over against all of our relativities. He is the norm by which we measure what we are and do. Christians, at least, should not lay this portrait of potential man aside and wander off into vain speculations about their right to explore the good life apart from him and wholly on their own initiative.

There is an interesting and fruitful verse in the fifth chapter of the Gospel of John: "The Father judges no one, but has given all judgment to the Son." Jesus Christ, then, does not pass judgment or pronounce judgment; he is judgment. There is a steadiness in him to which we can return to recover our own equilibrium when we are dizzy from the whir and whirl of life. He is the index to life as it should be. And he is judgment of our lives as they are. "Here is the man," said Pilate. Yes, here is *the* man, and we should not forget it.

Moreover, the love that is indispensable to authentic morality—that love which desires and empowers oneness—is not a natural human trait or a learned art; it is given and it has its source in God, the giver. "We love," says the First Letter of John, "because he first loved us." This does not mean that our love is reciprocal or that it expresses our gratitude. It means rather that our love is enabled by his. Apart from the God who is love, man does not love and cannot love, for love is of God. The power is not in us but in the God who wills all things to be one. Authentic morality, as we have defined it, is for man in his aloneness an impossibility. It places a huge responsibility on man, but it does not deprive him of that power that is beyond him—the love given in Christ.

Authentic morality then focuses on people to produce persons, a process that requires freedom as an indispensable climate and a love that is more than all loves as its standard and energy. This love, perfectly revealed to us in Jesus Christ, has its origin in the God who is love. We are asking, therefore, what effect the media of mass communication have on authentic morality, particularly on the transformation of people into persons.

3
The Uses of Mass Media

We have now pinned down one of the two definitions indispensable to an understanding of the effect of mass communication on authentic morality. Authentic morality, we have discovered, is not moralistic correctness or legalistic obedience to external and inflexible authorities. Rather, we have defined authentic morality as that human behavior that permits and encourages people to be persons within the bounds of the freedom and love God wills and provides for man. Since we are asking how mass media affect this kind of morality, it is essential that we know precisely what we mean by "mass media," our shorthand phrase for the various agencies of mass communication.

What do we mean by "communication"? In what relative or radical way does the word change when we add the modifier "mass"? What are the direct and the indirect impacts, the social and cultural influences, the educational and psychological consequences of this century's new forms of communication? In what way does mass communication shape for good or ill the human freedom that is indispensable to the development of real persons? These are some of the questions that now confront us.

The dictionary definition of communication gives us the quickest answer to the simplest of these questions, but we must go beyond that answer. The dictionary says that "communication," from the Latin word *communicare,* means to make common, to share, to impart, to transmit. So the concept of mass is intrinsic to the concept of communication. The principal idea in the word is that what is given to one is by him transmitted to many. We can communicate diseases, and we speak properly of communicable diseases. Military men refer to communications for troops and supplies and by this word mean the routes by which troops and supplies are moved.

But we are using the more general meaning of the word: the conveying and receiving of knowledge, ideas, impressions, ideologies, emotions. So the word takes us out of the physical realm into that area where men transmit their mental and spiritual possessions. It is by communication that the ideas, data, and feelings that are present in one person become present or available to more than one person.

The ability to communicate occurs in all forms of animal life. A solitary ant discovers the strawberry ice cream my granddaughter drops on the patio and in a short time there is on the spot a caravan of ants transporting the sweet stuff to headquarters. Somehow the exciting news is transmitted from one ant to another. Bees are reported to be even more phenomenal in relaying messages. But man excels all other forms of animal life in the ability to communicate. Man can transmit to man not only hard fact but also abstract thought and feeling. Since this ability is exceedingly limited in single-celled animal life, since it is one of the classifications by which we can distinguish lowly developed from highly developed forms of life, since man's powers of communication are unique in the animal kingdom, we can conclude that the ability to communicate is one of the marks of the full man God is creating. Therefore communication at its highest reaches has a moral and spiritual significance apart from its good or bad effects. We may argue about the kind and quality of communication, but we cannot argue against communication as such. We can demand better communication, but if we want man to be fully man, if we want people to be persons, we cannot demand less communication.

Potentially, then, whatever increases the sharing, transmitting and imparting of knowledge, ideas, and feelings is good and whatever decreases this sharing is bad. The easier communication between men becomes, the greater the opportunity for human beings to be human. True man is par excellence a communicating animal. The fact that this ability can be put to evil purposes does not alter it as a mark of his superiority in the animal world.

God is also a communicator. The Bible has sometimes been described as a chronicle of relationships: God with man, man with God, man with his neighbor, man with himself. The Bible could similarly be summarized as a recording of communications: conversations between God and his children, between man and man, and within the meditating hearts of solitary men; mighty acts by which God revealed his judgment and his mercy and the responsive acts by which man accepted or rejected the revealed will of God; the signs of God and the gestures of men. This dialogue in words and deeds rose at times to pitches so high that the descriptive word "communication" had to give way to the word "communion"—God and man in communion in the inner parts of their being. But the word "communion"—the best title for the Lord's supper—means communication at its highest reaches, at a level beyond physical media.

Communication is what the God of the Bible does best and superlatively in Christ. Communication, rising toward communion, is what man at his best does. Therefore when we discuss communication we have a religious, a moral and spiritual, rather than a technological theme.

It is well to remember, however, that at the moment we are thinking about communication itself rather than about the media and content of communication. Someone has said that words are devices by which we conceal thought. They can be used to confuse rather than clarify situations, to withhold rather than transmit information, to keep people from thinking rather than to enable them to think. If this is true of words, it is also true of all other media by which man relates himself to man. They can be perverted to purposes exactly opposite to those for which they were created. There are journals of the extreme right and the far left that technically have to be classified as media of communication, but they isolate the minds of their readers from the facts and seal them against the truth.

Advertisers often use radio and television not to give the public information about their product but to create a hunger and the false implication that their product will satisfy that hunger. Cigarette advertisers are notoriously culpable in the use of media to divert the public from the dangers of their product and to leave with viewers and listeners the impression that their product is in fact healthful. Dictators who control the media in their countries absolutely can saturate the air with propaganda to mold the minds of the people, with entertainment that diverts the people from a political or social crisis, or with patently false information. Hitler's use of radio to terrorize neighboring states and to dominate the minds and moods of Germans is a classic illustration of the perversion of media.

We must distinguish, therefore, between communication, which is beneficial to man and usually desirable, and the media of communication, which are merely instruments and which can be put to good uses or bad.

I said "usually desirable" because communication itself—the transmitting of ideas, feelings, and information—can, like the media, be corrupted to uses harmful to man. I am thinking of the plots hatched by thieves, the assignations arranged by panderers, the intrigues fashioned by politicians to bilk the people, the secret agreements by which nations exploit nations and betray peace. All of these are wholly dependent on man's ability to communicate with man. So man has as one of his highest properties an extraordinary capacity for communication. He is nature's best sender and receiver. This ability can help him become fully man—a truly moral creature—or it can be the instrument by which he compounds his woes. But communication itself is indispensable to the man-becoming-fully-man process.

Two men in our time have given extraordinary, poetic stress to man's need for communication.

Martin Buber, probably more than any other man in our era, saw the spiritual dimension of communication as the bridge between diverse groups. He knew that the decisive test of brotherhood is not within the community "but at the boundary between community and community, people and people, church and church, for this is the place where diversity of kind and mind is felt most strongly. Every time we stand this test, a new step is taken toward a new humanity, gathered in the name of God."

Dag Hammarskjöld, sharing this concern, stressed also the danger that the lines between men would be perverted to their destruction. In an address at Cambridge University in June, 1960, he said: "The human world is today as never before split into two camps, each of which understands the other as the embodiment of falsehood and itself as the embodiment of truth. . . . Hence one may foresee in the future a degree of reciprocity in mistrust where speech will turn into dumbness and sense into madness. . . . Only as there are men and women willing to step out of the opposing camps in the world, out of divergent groups in community life, and meet as men under God, and communicate, listen, speak with intent to understand can real dialogue ensue."

These men understood the urgent need for genuine communication dedicated to increasing the humanity of man and increasing his chances for survival.

What we have said thus far is that man's extraordinary ability to share, impart, transmit, and receive facts, ideas, and emotions is in its degree one of the marks that distinguishes him from all other creatures. We have acknowledged that this capacity for communication can be turned to man's destruction. We insist nevertheless that whatever increases man's powers of communication is good and that whatever decreases those powers is bad. We have also admitted that all media of communication are vulnerable to corruption by man to purposes that do not contribute to the creation of persons, but we have insisted that these instruments can be beneficial to authentic morality. We have noted that the word "communication" is a synonym for those relationships that we encounter under other descriptions in the Bible and in Christian theology. We know, therefore, that in discussing communication we are dealing with a subject central rather than tangential to our Christian faith. Against this background we can now place some more specific thoughts about the media of communication.

As long as man has been man he has had numerous means for transmitting his thoughts and feelings: nonverbal sounds, gestures, oral and written words, facial expressions, signs, monuments, drums, smoke signals, tunes, tapestries, carvings, paintings. The new factor in our time—mass media—vastly increases the range and speed of many of these old media.

In the past the user of the spoken word could, under favorable circumstances, be seen by a hundred thousand people and heard by perhaps twenty thousand. Now via television he can be seen and heard instantaneously by hundreds of millions of people. If man's progress in this field continues uninterrupted by war or by natural calamity the time will soon come when every person on earth can simultaneously watch and listen to the same "live" program. The first giant steps toward that probability were taken by transcontinental and transoceanic radio more than a generation ago.

I can recall how the immediacy of both hope and terror gripped us when in the 1930's and 1940's we listened to Winston Churchill's confident and resolute voice and to the rantings of Hitler and company. Now, satellites relay images as well as sounds across the Atlantic almost instantaneously.

This new phenomenon—man's ability to communicate instantaneously with multiplied millions of people—had its beginning in the Industrial Revolution, 1750 to 1850. This era in man's history first produced what we now call the slow media of mass communication: newspapers, journals, and books produced in such volume that they could be spread generally and regularly among the people. These slow media will remain, despite the direful predictions of the sensationalist Marshall McLuhan, about whom more will be said later. Then, about the middle of the nineteenth century, man began developing what we now call the fast or instantaneous media: telegraph, telephone, radio, motion pictures, and television. All of the fast media could also be called electronic media. To the mass communication already in existence they added two new factors: range and speed. They are not radically new but are the latest developments in man's effort to extend the scope of his senses.

The development of electronic media has experienced fantastic acceleration in this century. People fortunate enough to be as old as I am and to have lived as I have in the technologically most advanced and most retarded areas of this country have sensed, as others cannot, the wonder of this electronic progress.

As a young child I lived on a farm wholly isolated from all mass media, slow or fast. Now I am engulfed by both. When I was ten years old and had moved to town my mother sent me to a neighbor's house—the one with the telephone—with this instruction: "Take the black thing off the hook; hold it to your ear. A voice will say 'Number, please.' You say, 'Number nine.' Then another voice will say, 'Atlantic Coastline Railroad.' Then you say, 'What time is it?' When the voice tells you what time it is, run home as fast as you can and tell me."

Forty-four years later, from a distance of two thousand miles, I direct-dialed Area Code 312, number MI 3-0800, exchange 4103, and the line was busy. We have made fantastic progress! During world series time we boys used to gather with the men in a blocked off street before the Florence Hotel and watch the reports of the game's progress come in by telegram long after the contest was over. As I write this, golfing fans in England, Wales, Scotland, and Ireland are watching the final round of the U. S. Open at the Baltusrol Club in New Jersey as it is played and immediately relayed to them by television. When I was fourteen years old my father and I walked seven miles through the country in the depths of the night to see whether my dying grandfather was still living. Today man sends messages to and receives mechanically produced messages from the nearby planets in our solar system. We have indeed made wondrous progress in electronic communication.

In the United States, Canada, Europe, and Japan, twentieth-century progress in communication includes not only phenomenal increases in speed and range of senders but also an almost universal distribution of receivers. In the United States—the country with which we are particularly concerned—mass communication moves toward the level of universal communication. In an article titled "Mass Communication Trends" in the April 15, 1962, issue of *Concern,* Russell B. Bomberger gives us a statistical picture of the extent to which the mass media saturate this country. According to Bomberger, 110,000,000 Americans read a newspaper every day, and 20,000,000 homes receive a weekly magazine; 98 percent of the homes have radios, and 86 percent have television sets. Seven out of ten Americans see at least one feature movie a year. More than one-half billion books are bought in the United States every year, not counting textbooks.

Bomberger's estimate of the number of radios and television sets in the United States seems excessive but in the second edition of his book *Freedom and Communications* (University of Illinois Press), Dan Lacy gives a similar picture: "There were 87,800,000 radio sets and 49,300,000 television receivers in the United States by 1958; 97 percent of all homes had radios, most of them two or more, and 83 percent had television sets, with the latter figure rising rapidly. These household sets were augmented by 53 million portable and automobile radios, so that almost no American needed ever to be beyond the flow of broadcast words and images. About 3,200 radio stations and 500 television stations provided a continuous service, reaching with radio into every corner, and with television into almost every corner, of the United States."

Although the telephone lacks some of the characteristics of mass communication common to radio and television, the telephone industry has also had an extraordinary growth in the past generation. In *Concern's* April 15, 1962, emphasis on communications, Senator John O. Pastore of Rhode Island noted that in the last four decades the population of the United States has grown 60 percent, but the number of telephones has expanded 500 percent.

One of the Roman emperors—Caligula, I believe—wished that all of the Romans had one neck so that he could wring all of the people's necks at once. At the rate we are going the American people will soon all have one eye and one ear, for all of them can even now be exposed to one sight and one sound simultaneously. This situation is not as ideal for the dictator as the one Caligula desired, but we must not assume that a society in which the attention of the whole people can be focused on one subject is inevitably a good one.

During this period in which the fast media have spread their influence rapidly over the whole country the slow media have done little more than hold their own. Daily newspapers dwindled from nearly two thousand separate publications thirty years ago to less than eighteen hundred today. The number of general interest magazines dropped since World War II from 335 in 1946 to 186 in 1960. Circulation increased but only in proportion to the rise in population. Proportionately there are no more people in the United States reading newspapers today than there were twenty-five years ago. And, says Lacy, "the dissemination of news and other editorial content per capita is certainly relatively and, probably absolutely, less than in prewar years." Nevertheless, it is much too early to say, as McLuhan and others do, that we have entered the age of the postliterate man. The shaking-down process has just begun, and we shall not know until another generation has passed whether the fast media put the slow ones out of business.

There is, I suppose, no way of knowing exactly how much time the average American gives to mass media. The amount of dedicated time given exclusively to radio, television, and reading could be calculated with a fair degree of accuracy, but most Americans have learned to divide their attention between the media and the task at hand. Housewives, in many cases, turn on their television sets in the morning, leave them on all day, and arrange their work so that they pass through the area of reception periodically. High school students insist that they study best when their radios are going constantly and full blast. I am sure that my sixteen-year-old son has rigged his room so that his radio turns on full volume when he enters his room, but unfortunately his apparatus—whatever it is—does not turn off his radio when he departs. And, I must confess, I never watch television myself without a book in my hand and a writing pad in my lap. My Protestant conscience will not let me do otherwise. So, many of us give the media a divided attention, while others sit stupefied before the instruments hour after hour.

A reasonable guess is that radio, television, films, and reading consume thirty-five hours a week of the average American's time; and, television increasingly gets the lion's share of this time. This means that the average American gives the mass media 15 percent of his total time, a period of his life equal to what he gives his job and nearly ten times more hours than the regular communicant gives his church. Even if the content absorbed in such long stretches of sedentary reception were entirely wholesome and creative it would still be wise to ask whether so much passivity, so much absorbed but unused data, so much generated but unexpended emotion diminishes rather than increases man's being fully man.

Don Lacy, in the work already mentioned, put the problem thus:

"The average American remains 'plugged in' to his culture for a major part of all his free hours, receiving an endless flow of entertainment and information. . . . Indeed, so massive and continuous is his exposure to communication that a new set of problems is created, relating not to the 'under-reception' of information but rather to 'over-reception' to such a degree that vicarious experience dominates direct experience and the uncritical acceptance of a projected image may drown out the development of autonomous judgment and cultural individuality."

I do not fear knowledge and I assume that Lacy would agree that man cannot know too much. Nor do I fear entertainment. But I do fear undigested knowledge that is not in some way translated into experience. When man becomes a repository for undifferentiated data that is not in some way converted into his becoming a person and enabling other people to be persons, he resembles a machine more than he does a man. Man is fundamentally a "being," not a "knowing." His knowing must be instrumental to his being, and his being includes action and involvement.

Entertainment is a service and activity, beneficial to man even when it is merely a diversion that for a time takes man away from himself, revives him, and gives him a freshened perspective of himself. In an article in the April 20, 1966, issue of *The Christian Century*—"What Is Christian Art?"—Jane and John Dillenberger showed how absurd Leo Tolstoy was when he insisted that good works of art must communicate ideas that express the uniting of men with God and with one another. By this test Tolstoy rejected as bad art "most of the music of Beethoven, Haydn, Mozart, and Schubert; Dante's *Divine Comedy;* the greater part of Shakespeare's and Goethe's works; and his own earlier writings."

The Dillenbergers were correct in suggesting that art in all its forms is its own excuse for being. True art does not have to do anything or say anything. It *is.* Similar words can be written about entertainment. There is bad entertainment, of course; but good entertainment does not have to be aesthetically perfect or moralistically good. Many Christians, even in this day, are under the spell of a neurotic compulsion to find a moral in every form of entertainment or feel guilty for having indulged themselves in it.

This is absurd. Entertainment that has no moralistic or educational value but which simply entertains is greatly to be preferred as a temporary escape from oneself and one's problems to numerous other ways by which men duck the hard challenges of life. We should neither resent nor contest the fact that the mass media provide escapist literature, films, and broadcasts.

But a good thing can become bad when the consumption of it is inordinate. A temporary escape from oneself—from familiar and beloved company, from life's burdens—is good; a permanent escape is bad. The vast amount of escapist entertainment available to Americans today threatens to turn them into parasites, into cultural schizoids, into entertainment addicts who are not temporarily but usually disoriented. The television knob has the compelling fascination for some hands that the bottle has for others. When you are frustrated, when you conclude that you can't "do" yourself, it is tempting to turn on the machine and watch pictures of someone else "doing."

This is the hazard—that innocuous escapist entertainment will become for most Americans an increasing and unbreakable addiction that gradually diminishes them as persons. And this danger increases as the media more and more dominate the culture and as more and more people spend more and more time glued to receivers. Since most of our broadcasting is commercially based and since the lifetime of a program, a journal, or a newspaper is dependent on the popularity of the content distributed, the trend is for disseminators to offer the people increased and addictive doses of escapist entertainment.

Mass communication will inevitably strive for mass appeal. Left to run their natural course, the media will substitute entertainment for knowledge and thought and will displace the artistically, culturally, and religiously best forms of entertainment with the escapism that appeals to the least common denominator of the public. And the gravest aspect of this danger is not what is broadcast by the media but what must necessarily be excluded by the media when the time available for broadcasting is preempted by light entertainment. Programs that have a high quality of educational, religious, ideological, and polemical content cannot contend successfully for the attention of the listener and the viewer when they are matched with lavishly financed programs that appeal to man's desire to be entertained.

We now need to answer two closely related but nevertheless dissimilar questions: What are the effects of mass media on the culture of a people? And, what are the effects of the *content* of mass media on authentic morality? It is important to see that these are two different questions demanding separate answers. In the first case, we are asking what impact the media have on society apart from their message. Here we are treating the mass media—particularly the fast, electronic media—as we would the cotton gin, the automobile, the atomic bomb, the computer, or the miracle drugs. Each of these inventions reshaped culture and society profoundly, even though none of them is a medium. They helped change ideas, restructure social patterns, jeopardize and safeguard our physical life.

We should subject electronic communication to the same kind of analysis that we would apply to these other instruments. Then we should ask what is known about the effect of the content of mass media on man's struggle to be fully human and whether—and if so, how—a particular medium gives a peculiar flavor to a specific content. Is there, for example, an intrinsic difference between a message transmitted by one of the slow media and that same message transmitted by one of the fast media? Which has the most authority, a book or a television drama? Which gives to a particular message the most lasting impact, a journal or a motion picture? And—applying our definition of authentic morality—does the content broadcast by the mass media focus on people or on money and institutions? Does it seek and encourage and enable the transformation of people into persons or is it dehumanizing? Does the broadcast content free man or imprison him? Does it profane the love that wills wholeness for man or honor and aid that love that is beyond all sectarian limitations but is known to us Christians in Jesus Christ?

However much some of us may now want to do so, it is impossible to ignore Marshall McLuhan and his book *Understanding Media* in our attempt to answer the first question—the impact of mass media on culture and society apart from the impact of their content. Marshall McLuhan was formerly a teacher of English at Toronto University and a director of the Center for Culture and Technology. In September, 1967, he assumed the Albert Schweitzer chair in humanities at Fordham University. The publication of his book *Understanding Media,* in 1964, marked for his more fanatical devotees the beginning of an era to be compared in importance with the discovery of America or the first atomic explosion. McLuhan's dispassionate critics, however, say that he merely rephrases in an exciting way what sounder and soberer scholars have been declaring about our electronic age for some time; that he is a sloganeer, a preacher, an intellectual "con man" who captivates you with his language but puts worthless strips of newspaper in the bag he exchanges for your trust; that he picks up a few sparkling grains of truth and tries to build a continent out of them; that he proclaims his modesty but presents his theories with an arrogant insinuation that they are of course infallible. Having read his master work, listened to him lecture, and watched him bungle as he attempted to field sharp questions from his audience, I feel—as Michael J. Arlen said in the April 1, 1967, *New Yorker*—that McLuhan "keeps skittering all over the place. Maybe, one day, he'll settle for something less."

McLuhanism, in my opinion, is a great deal of error mixed with some truth for which the author claims too much. One of his favorite phrases, for example, is that "the medium is the message," by which he means that the medium has more impact and is therefore more important than its content, that the medium in itself determines what we are to become and that its content is therefore relatively unimportant. Thus he takes a partly true premise—media influence us apart from their content—and moves with it toward a wholly false conclusion; i.e., we should concentrate our attention and our study on the media rather than on their content. He believes that the way we react to television or computers is far more important than what is on them or in them.

About this point, Arlen wrote in a *New Yorker* article "The Air—Marshall McLuhan and the Technological Embrace": "It's hard to forget that the first thing that boring old Gutenberg printed was the Bible and the first thing television gave us was Uncle Miltie—and, on present evidence, there doesn't seem to be any very pressing basis for tossing out the first because of the second."

McLuhan would have helped us, rather than stifling discussion, if he had merely said—as is true—that the media have an influence beyond their content. But as Father John M. Culkin of Fordham University—one of McLuhan's fans—said, McLuhan feels that he must make "the truth stand on its head to attract attention."

Another of McLuhan's major points is that electronic communication has put the printed word out of business, that electronic man is necessarily postliterate man, that we can no longer depend on the printed page and the verbal forms of communication. Moreover he expresses a strong distrust for the linear patterns that underlie the way man has, since the beginning of civilization, perceived and described his world. In the past, perception and expression have moved in a line; the images have had a sequential relation.

When we learn from the printed page, our eyes move from left to right or from right to left and our thoughts, similarly, are linear. But, says McLuhan, the electronic media have ended all that by giving to cognition, perception, and expression an all-at-once quality. And this way, he says, is better. You don't read about Ruby's shooting Lee Oswald in a narrated newspaper account; you see it on television; you become a part of the scene, a part of the action. This is the way preliterate man learned, the way primitive and backward people like the Eskimos learn. And, says McLuhan, this better way of learning the electronic media make possible.

A number of hands go up begging for a chance to refute McLuhan at this point and we can recognize only a few of them. Arlen is one who will have to be heard. He wrote: "Art, after all, imitates life, and life is surely, among other things, intrinsically geometric. Nature is geometric. Trees, tides, plants, planets don't move psychedelically; they move geometrically. And as long as nature exists in any recognizable form the paths of force and tension and, consequently, the order that man intuitively responds to will in the main be linear, too."

Second, McLuhan apparently forgets that all of us have all-at-once learning and communicating experiences every day. We have not had to wait for the advent of electronics for this opportunity. This kind of learning has always been a part of the human experience. Man has neatly blended this learning and communicating process with the linear processes.

Third, the linear processes basic to literate thought produced the Bible, the Taj Mahal, Shakespeare's *Hamlet,* Beethoven's *Ninth Symphony,* Dostoevski's *The Brothers Karamazov,* Michelangelo's *Pieta,* and they produced the electronic media. Processes of thought that have achieved such a record do not have to defer to the thought processes of preliterate man nor to those of Eskimos.

Fourth, the man who has come among us announcing the death of literate man and the demise of his instrument—the printed word—refutes himself by what should be for him most embarrassing behavior. When he wants to spread his gospel of the triumph of electronics over print, he publishes a book! McLuhan achieves his best presentation of his theses in the linear and printed form and is—as I have observed personally—surprisingly, embarrassingly inadequate when he approaches the public through any other media or on the lecture platform. I agree with Eric Hoffer—the longshoreman who works on the docks, teaches at college level, and publishes books—when he says that if McLuhan doesn't believe in the printed word he should "leave books to hell alone."

Nevertheless, there is truth in McLuhan's argument that the media change society, and it will be well for us to forget McLuhan's excessive claims and see what that truth is. Harvey Cox—leaning on McLuhan's thought—said in a November 25, 1964, article in *The Christian Century*—"The Gospel and Postliterate Man"—that "when the technology of communications media changes there is a concomitant change in the culture's way of perceiving reality." But in a society in which the educational process depends primarily on the printed word, in which 110 million people read a newspaper every day, in which 20 million homes receive magazines each week, and in which 500 million books plus textbooks are sold each year, where is "postliterate man"? Cox's postliterate man is as elusive as his secular man. It is hard to find a genuine example. But, as with McLuhan, so with Cox: there is some truth in what he says and we need to find it. It may be true that the new media will make deep and lasting changes in psychological man, but it is much too early to make even an intelligent guess about that. Certainly we must avoid elevating hunches into sociological and psychological dogma, and we should be wary of those who do. We shall look then for those demonstrable changes the fast media make in society.

I detect three such changes that can be identified and demonstrated.

First, by their saturation of the whole country, the mass media will have a universalizing effect on our culture and on our society. Regional differences in language, accent, dress, taste, political bias, and sectarian allegiance will gradually disappear under the daily blows of media that knock off the distinguishing edges of our sectionalism. All of these differences—most of them superficial—are the products of isolation.

What the automobile, the airplane, and widespread industrialization began, general and instantaneous communication will finish—the elimination of the hinterland, of rural areas, of cultural and religious enclaves. I suppose the Amish people and perhaps a few other sects will barricade themselves against the media's invasion, but the barricades will fall. Recently in a popular magazine we saw pictures of Amish youth listening surreptitiously to transistor radios. In the cultural sense there is no longer a rural America, no longer pockets where you find strange customs and people unacquainted with what occurs in the rest of the world, no longer a lag between what is said in New York, Chicago, or Los Angeles and its repetition in West Virginia, Wyoming, or Mississippi. What is worn on the streets of New York City one day will be seen on the streets of Butte, Montana, the next. The latest musical fad, the newest joke, the wildest hairdos, spread with the speed of light by the electronic media, seem to appear simultaneously in every part of the country. The mass media, then, will for good or ill eliminate a great part of this country's cultural plurality.

We can expect, moreover, that the mass media will also and simultaneously universalize this nation's mores at a deeper level than its customs, that they will eliminate regional codes of morality and put general ones in their places. It was correctly assumed in the past that the behavioral patterns of the rural areas of the country would be more conservative, more traditional, more pietistic than those of the metropolitan areas. Let us take one illustration.

When I grew up in the South there was in fact a southern way of life. It included not only certain racial attitudes and conduct but also a distinct southern morality that was a generous blend of religion, gentility, propriety, ancestor worship, and tradition. This distinctiveness was made possible by the relative isolation of the South from the rest of the country. Largely agricultural; saturated with the ingrown, self-conscious attitudes characteristic of a people defeated in war; heavily barricaded from within by those social structures that would close it off from threats to its racial patterns; burying its slender but strong liberal tradition and its social conscience under heavy concentrations on the externalities and trivia of religion—these were the unhappy characteristics of a region voluntarily and involuntarily isolated from the rest of the nation.

But the products of this isolation were not all bad. If the regionalism of the South has to be blamed for certain unfortunate developments in the area, it must also be credited with some of the distinctive and fortunate developments. The human relationships in this section of the country were in the time of its isolation characterized by a warmth, openness, and genuine concern for the other person that were not matched anywhere else in the nation.

"Southern hospitality" was a euphemism for something that ran much deeper than mere hospitality—an authentic interest in the other person as person. I shall never forget how shocked I was when, at the age of sixteen, I first visited New York City and discovered there a cold indifference for people as people. Defensive façades were drawn like heavy curtains between person and person, the absence of affinity in the presence of staggering proximity. Eight years later I lived there and learned that the free, easy, open human relations that I had experienced in the southern town were an impossibility in the northern metropolis. (This fact has staggering implications for community as more and more we become a conurbated people packed in the great metropolitan areas.) Although the South was a long time isolated from the rest of the nation, southerners were not isolated from one another.

Moreover it is no accident that the South has been, until recently, the reservoir out of which the nation's churches in other parts of the country have drawn clergymen to make up their own deficiency. The story may never be told, because the statistics may not be available. But it is a fact, nevertheless, that the South has supplied not only ministers for its own churches but also ministers for those northern and western churches that have not produced their own leadership. It also can be shown that the South has produced an inordinate part of the civil rights leadership of the nation, Negro and white. This surplus supply of religious and social leaders could not have developed in a spiritual vacuum. It came, rather, out of a cultural setting in which people took their religion—whatever its deficiencies—seriously.

This south began to break up in the early 1930's. It has not gone but it is going rapidly, and the mass media hasten the process. For good or ill, one of the victims will be the South's distinctive morality, its religious way of life. The mass media will swiftly amalgamate the regional moralities of the country, universalizing the moral standards and tastes. Whether this also means a leveling effect, a pulling of the moral tone down to the least common denominator, or whether it means an elevating of moral consciousness and conduct, we cannot at this point say. For that depends on the content broadcast by the media. What we are saying now is that one of the certain results of universal broadcasting and receiving will be a universalizing of customs, concepts, and conduct.

Second, the mass media have a liberating effect on great masses of the people, freeing them especially from prisons of ignorance. Perhaps we can see this better if we first take an illustration from outside our own country. What has caused "the rising tides of expectation" in South America, Africa, and Asia? What has produced in these repressed and underdeveloped countries the new and in some cases revolutionary surges toward nationalism and toward popular control of the government? These questions reach deep into great complexities; no single answer will do. But there is one answer that cannot be omitted if the whole truth is to be known. The mass media—first the radio and increasingly television—have opened the minds of the three-quarters of the people isolated from the world and ignorant of what goes on in the world to the way the other quarter—North America and Europe—lives. This awakening has transformed depressed and despairing people into depressed and aspiring people.

In Cuba I saw crowds of *campesinos* gathered in the plazas to watch the local, municipally-owned television set. In the Negev in Israel I saw a Bedouin riding a camel, reading a book, and listening to a transistor radio. In a theater in India I watched a filmed report of Nehru's visit to the United States a short time after it happened. It will never again be possible to tell these people that life cannot be better for them. They have seen with their own eyes and heard with their own ears about a life that surpasses their dreams but that is commonplace for other men.

To a lesser but significant degree this development occurs in our own country. The repressed people in Mississippi and Alabama, the depressed people in Appalachia, the migrant workers, and the Indians on reservations have been introduced by the mass media to ways of life which a generation ago they had difficulty imagining. I recall several songs sung during World War I, one of which had this line: "How you gonna keep 'em down on the farm after they've seen Paree?" The question now is, "How you gonna keep 'em down anywhere after they've seen TV?"

The mass media, opening the eyes and ears of the people to the world, are a powerful incentive, producing in Americans as well as in people everywhere else rising and irresistible tides of expectation. When the encyclopedic record of the Negro's rise in this country is finally compiled, there should be a list of the blunders made, from their point of view, by the racists.

I can name three of the mistakes that racists have made that turned out for the good of the Negro: They gave the Negro the Bible in the hope that it would make him docile; they sold him secondhand automobiles for an exorbitant profit; and, for the same reason let him buy radio and television sets on the instalment plan. Thus they gave the Negro the religion that would not let him be satisfied with anything less than being a man; gave him the mobility that extended his escape from slavery to a world of freedom and prosperity vastly different from his own.

Since, as we have said, freedom is the required climate for the production of real persons—authentic morality—then we have to view the mass media as agents of genuine morality wherever they liberate man from ignorance about himself, about his condition, and about other men. Certainly, to a great extent, the electronic media in this country deserve honors for flooding the man imprisoned by ignorance with liberating and challenging data. They have not of course removed the occasions for his misery, but they have assured him that these occasions need not be permanent. They have taught him—intentionally or not—that he can be hopeful rather than fatalistic about his life and the lives of his loved ones. They have broken open to him a new world—sometimes fictional and fantastic, of course—toward which he can struggle with some hope for success.

I suspect in the third place that mass media will have an integrating effect on our society and perhaps eventually on the world. The massive and instantaneous lines of communication will free the several parts of the country from their regional isolation and, beyond that, knit them together in a single fabric. A people who can move about the country as freely, easily, and quickly as Americans can, who read the same magazines, listen to the same radio programs, watch the same events portrayed on television will inevitably develop a strong consciousness of mutual identity. Whether this identity produces a deadly uniformity or not depends on the content of the media themselves. The media as media cannot be held responsible for that. They are the cords that lace the country together. What men say to each other over the long distance telephone lines, the coaxial cables, the radio and television antennae, the nationally syndicated newspaper columns, and the weekly journals is a matter of great urgency and consequence. But the media as instruments give us the opportunity to develop an enriched and strengthened sense of people, of folk and community, of national solidarity.

As mass communication becomes worldwide, it can serve in this larger sphere—if its content will permit it to do so—to make the peoples of the world conscious of their oneness, of their common problems and mutual perils, of their necessary interdependence in solving their problems and avoiding their perils. International communication by way of electronically equipped satellites is now in its most primitive beginnings. In a few years Early Bird will be as out-of-date as the hand-cranked telephone now is.

We are just entering the near side of a vast new era of intercontinental and interplanetary communication that can usher in the blessings or unleash the curses of human compactness. One of the most hopeful events that occurred during the 1967 explosion in the Middle East was the use of the "hot line" between Moscow and Washington. It is possible that during this crisis the whole world would have blown apart if that instantaneous and direct communication had not been possible. Transmissions facilities are now as important to peace as good intentions.

In these three respects, then, and probably in others that do not occur to us now, mass media will, as modern instruments, reshape our culture and our society. They will universalize customs and moralities, liberate man from his emotional and intellectual ghettos, and integrate man's scattered societies into one vast communications system.

Our second question asks about the impact of the content of media on consumers. Let us first raise this question about the media in general and then take up more leisurely an examination of the content of such specific media as radio and television, the printed word, and motion pictures. Although the judicial and legislative fields are not properly described as media of communication, they do have a profound influence on morality. We should therefore include these forces and note in what respect they contribute to or detract from true morality.

What, then, is the effect of mass communication as distinct from its instruments on people and on their becoming or ceasing to be real persons? Let me admit at once that men like Marshall McLuhan have given us some interesting and provocative hypotheses. They have helped to break up our caked patterns of thought about the sharing of facts, feelings, and ideas. But their hypotheses are merely educated hunches and should not be received as though they were divine revelations or proved theories.

The fact is that we still know very little about the effect of radio, television, and motion pictures on personality and character. Everybody, for example, talks about the effects of television and radio on children. Almost everybody has an opinion. These opinions range from one extreme to the other; but, as yet, no one actually knows on the basis of clinical studies and scientific surveys what radio, television, and motion pictures actually do to us beneath the surfaces of our being. My task here would be much easier if it were possible to refer to definitive and indisputable psychological analyses and sociological charts. But there are no such exhaustive and reliable resources to which we can turn. Our answers to these questions will also be educated hunches. And we must be modest about them. It may be that they will say more about our personal prejudices and about our traditions and presuppositions than they do about the effects of the media.

Even if we take the worst fare offered by television and motion pictures—that depicting crime, violence, and sensuality—we cannot be sure of its effect on the viewer or on viewers generally. We can imagine that such programs encourage imitation, that they school youth in delinquency, that they are the sparks that explode repressed criminality, that they debase human life. These may be valid suppositions, but they may not be. We have no data on which to rest such a conclusion. We may take—as some people do—an exactly opposite position, saying that such programs are escape valves, releasing tensions and hostilities that would otherwise become antisocial. This, too, may be a valid supposition; but in this case, too, we have no evidence sufficient for a solid and final judgment. We may say that the psychological effect of such programs depends entirely on what it meets within people—just as alcohol consumption or the use of LSD does—making some people delinquent and providing a vicarious release for potential delinquency in other people. This may be a valid supposition, but we cannot prove it.

Those who want to pursue this aspect of the problem still further should read *The Effects of Mass Communication* by Joseph T. Klapper (The Free Press of Glencoe, Illinois, 1960). With permission by the Macmillan Company, I quote the following introductory passage from pages two and three of this book:

Teachers, preachers, parents, and legislators have asked us a thousand times over these past fifteen years whether violence in the media produces delinquency, whether the escapist nature of much of the fare does not blind people to reality, and just what the media can do to the political persuasions of their audiences. To these questions we have not only failed to provide definitive answers, but we have done something worse: we have provided evidence in partial support of every hue of every view. We have claimed, on the one hand, and on empirical grounds, that escapist material provides its audience with blinders and with an unrealistic view of life, and on the other hand, that it helps them meet life's real problems. We have hedged on the crime and violence question, typically saying, "Well, probably there is no causative relationship, but there just might be a triggering effect." In reference to persuasion, we have maintained that the media are after all not so terribly powerful, and yet we have reported their impressive successes in promoting such varied phenomena as religious intolerance, the sale of war bonds, belief in the American Way, and disenchantment with Boy Scout activities. It is surely no wonder that a bewildered public should regard with cynicism a research tradition which supplies, instead of definitive answers, a plethora of relevant but inconclusive and at times seemingly contradictory findings.

Having entered these precautions, Klapper offers several tentative proposals, expressing the hope that further research will either modify them or prove them wrong altogether. Let me translate these tentative proposals from their technical language into words more characteristic of our study and add some comments that will, I hope, be faithful to his thought.

He suggests that mass communication is only one of several teaching situations to which children and adults are subjected, even in a society where the mass media have a primary claim on public attention. This means that mass communication is not in itself sufficiently influential to produce specific results. It is merely one of several contributory agents in the development of character and personality. The child, for example, learns from what his parents say and chiefly from what they do. He learns from his peers, from the community in which he lives, from his schoolteachers, from Sunday School and church, from newspapers and magazines—particularly the comics—and from television and radio. Obviously a child whose general learning situation is wholesome will react in one way to fare provided by the mass media, and a child whose general environment is bad will react in another. Sometimes parents, seeing antisocial behavior in their children, blame the cowboy and gangster pictures their children see in the movies and on television when they should blame themselves. Parental influence—particularly the parents' casual, unpremeditated words and deeds—remains the dominant molder of the character of children even in homes where radio and television sets run incessantly and programs are selected at random.

Klapper says further that we should consider the probability that the mass media tend to confirm and reinforce attitudes toward life rather than produce them or change them. It does not matter whether the particular attitude has to do with politics, international affairs, race relations, the use of violence, the value of life, the worth of persons, the mode of conduct proper in human relations. In each case, says this proposal, the media are more likely to reinforce than to change opinion.

I think this proposal should be tested in the light of the fact that advertisers spend billions of dollars to produce hungers and to change tastes for specific brands of cigarettes, beer, automobiles, and cosmetics. If it is true that the media merely reinforce previously formed opinion, then Madison Avenue squanders huge amounts of money provided by manufacturers to create a desire and a preference for their products. I doubt that manufacturers are so prodigal with their money. If commercials produce and change opinions then we should at least be suspicious of statements that the programs bought by manufacturers merely reinforce existent attitudes.

If it is correct to say that mass media merely reinforce existent opinion, consider the burden and the opportunity this fact presents to the Christian home and the church, to parents and the Sunday School. Are we laying down in our children at the very earliest ages permanent foundations on which they can stand poised and unshaken when the mass media assault them? Are we providing for our children fiber-building experiences, or are we surrendering them to electronic baby-sitters to be nursed day after day on pap?

Have we considered the possibility that the Sunday School, as we have known it in the past, is now an inefficient anachronism that should be replaced by an entirely new teaching situation? One of the gravest dangers of the advent of mass media is that they give us something new to blame for our failure as parents and teachers.

Perhaps it is true, however, that the more important a subject is to a listener or a viewer, the less influential the media are in changing his mind. John Crosby, television critic of the now defunct *New York Herald Tribune,* wrote some time ago: "It might be stated as Crosby's law that the more important the subject is, the less influence the guy with the mike has. In matters of the most profound importance to the individual—say, religion—I doubt that the Murrows, or Godfreys, the Winchells, or anyone else could sway a single soul a single inch." This may be true, but here again our judgment depends more on what we imagine to be the case than it does on solid evidence.

My personal opinion is that the more important the subject is to the consumer, the more likely it is that his opinion will be changed by indirection rather than by direction, by impression rather than by preaching—a probability to which our denominational and conciliar commissions on films, radio, and television should pay far more attention than they do.

I greatly admire Martin Luther King, Jr., and am confident that he will eventually be saluted by Negroes and whites alike as one of the great men of our century. Yet, I doubt that the appearance of King on radio or television changes many racial attitudes or much racial behavior. But the appearance of the Negro actor and humorist Bill Cosby on the television program "I Spy," in a heroic and highly sympathetic role in which he has a free and easy relation with a white companion and other whites, will, I believe, gradually change many racial prejudices. In the long run—and this is for religious people and civil rights leaders the irony of the situation—a Sidney Poitier, a Harry Belafonte, or a Johnny Mathis will do more to sweeten race relations, to equalize justice, and to improve the acceptance of Negroes in a white-dominated society than all the Stokely Carmichaels and the Floyd McKissicks—however important these latter figures may be as social catalysts. Through this medium, I am suggesting, we learn more by absorption than we do by indoctrination.

This being so, our churches still have a great deal to learn about the use of mass media in propagating the gospel. This is a field both too vast and, in some of its particulars, too tangential to our interests to be covered at this time. But I should in this setting make two suggestions to those people who, as Christians, want to use the mass media for evangelistic and educational purposes.

First, it is not wise to arbitrarily transfer a form of communication from one medium to another. As a rule, each form will require its own medium. Take preaching for example. Preaching ranks very high on, if not at the top of, my list of the ways to communicate the gospel. But preaching as we now know it is effective only in certain settings, only through certain media. Harry Emerson Fosdick, Ralph Sockman, and others proved a generation ago that preaching can be successful over radio if the preacher is extraordinarily competent. But no one has yet proved that preaching can be successful when broadcast by television, however competent the preacher may be. The televiewer naturally expects far more action than a preacher can or should provide. There are exceptions, of course, but as a rule the television time available to the churches should not be filled with televised church services or with sermons. It is far better for the churches to use such time for the broadcast of those programs of music, drama, art, and other forms that convey the Christian message indirectly rather than through indoctrination.

Although I do not share his enthusiasm for McLuhan, I believe that Alva I. Cox, Jr., staff associate for educational media in the National Council of Churches' department of educational development, was making the right point when he wrote the following in the article "Art, Technology and Education" in the July 6, 1966, issue of *The Christian Century:*

> Even where the new media are being accepted and used [by the churches] the verbal orientation has been imposed on them. When television is used, a Sunday School class is put on the air. When an experiment is conducted in programmed instruction, a book is programmed. New technological devices are looked upon as means of communicating rational-verbal ideas. This is illustrated in most

filmstrips: the primary emphasis is on words—the fundamental assumption is that pictures can illustrate the words. This is simply a new way of putting words together for communicating rational ideas. Great effort and discipline will be required if we are to free ourselves from our verbal commitments.

I accept this opinion, even though I do not agree with the implication that pictures are superior to words in communicating ideas. Anyone who does believe this should try putting John 3:16 into pictures. He will soon discover that the twenty-four words of this verse are better than ten thousand pictures. But it is a mistake to impose a format composed largely of words on a medium perfected to transmit images in motion, or—as far as sermons are concerned—to convey in written form what was constructed for oral delivery. Only preachers—and not many of them—read printed sermons.

Let me say also in this apparent digression that every medium and every form of communication will leave its own peculiar markings on the content it conveys, just as the barrel of a rifle marks and gives a twist to the bullet it projects. The form and the medium will in each instance impart something of its own nature to the content it transmits. Therefore, form and medium limit content.

The gospel is more than the best preaching of it. The greatest story ever told is far greater than the film *The Greatest Story Ever Told.* The film will inevitably diminish the fact. Said differently, this means that the gospel is too big, too important to be trusted to any form or to any medium. In a day in which competition for the ears and eyes of men grows ever keener, we must deputize every form and every medium for the proclamation and transmission of the good news of God's will and love in Jesus Christ. And as we do so we must learn from the artist and the technician what they have to teach us about the effective use of the new media.

These words are in fact no digression. Indeed, it is hypocritical to tremble before the possibly deleterious effects of the mass media on authentic morality and to complain about how the electronic media are demoralizing our children if we do not learn how to use new forms and new instruments in proclaiming and teaching and demonstrating our faith.

A long time ago Augustine said in his little work on preaching that it is folly for good men not to use for the service of the truth the instruments that bad men use so effectively for the service of falsehood. That is our situation as a Christian people. It is folly and sinful if we do not use for the sake of the gospel the skills and instruments that men indifferent to the gospel use so effectively to sell soap, smoke, and suds. All of the forms of communication are in the public domain. We can use them if we choose to use them, and we can learn how to use them well.

With some inconsequential exceptions, all of the mass media are privately owned. They do not belong to us. But the medium through which the mass media operate—the air—does belong to us. At the 1925 conference in Washington, a conference considering regulations for radio broadcasting, Herbert Hoover, then Secretary of Commerce, said: "The ether is a public medium and its use must be for the public interest." This view became and remains national policy. The churches should not jeopardize their right to the air either by failing to use it, by cluttering it with content poorly designed in form for this kind of communication, or by insisting that the media conform to sectarian and superficial codes of morality. Our Christian concern for authentic morality must necessarily include three other major concerns: how other people use the mass media, how we use them, and how we provide for our children and youth learning situations that reduce the dangers and increase the benefits of mass communication.

4

Censorship and Morality's Habitat

Some words in the English language have become almost inseparably wedded: ham and eggs, cup and saucer, salt and pepper. These combinations are convenient, but the more abstract the words, the more dangerously misleading the combination.

The word "censorship" and the word "obscenity" are strongly linked in the American mind. You rarely see or hear one without discovering the other lurking nearby. These words do have an affinity for each other, but each of them also has an independent existence and a distinct significance. It is therefore unfortunate that one of these words automatically makes us think of the other. Therefore, in this work I undertake the perhaps impossible task of cutting the link of popular thought which ties these words together and the even more difficult task of dealing separately with each of these words and its practical effects. We will explore now the varied effects of censorship on the freedom that is authentic morality's natural habitat and take up later the effects of obscenity and pornography.

The divorcing of these two words from each other is justified by the fact that each of them is imprecise, slippery, and hard to pin down. Obscenity, as we will note later in some detail, is the vaguer, the more elusive of the two subjects; but censorship as we commonly use the term is only slightly less so. Consequently, when we throw together these two loose-jointed words, we greatly compound the difficulty of understanding either one of them. Moreover, by constantly linking censorship with obscenity we create the impression that the controversy over freedom and restraint has to do only with man's sexuality. Few people will quarrel with the statement that man's sexuality is one of the dominant factors of his nature. Surely also all of us admit that for good or ill the sexual revolution is one of the crucial developments of our time. Nevertheless, man's freedom as a political and civil being has more elementary importance than his freedom as a sexual being. For man's sexual freedom and many of his other freedoms are wholly dependent on the range and bounds of his political and civil rights.

When censorship and obscenity are too closely and constantly identified with each other, two other dangers develop. There are people so afraid that man will abuse his sexuality—according to their narrow and sometimes morbid definition of sexual abuse—that they gladly surrender many primary political and civil freedoms in order to impose restrictions on what they think man should know and do as a sexual creature. And, the corollary fact is that autocratic men who want a closed society—a limitation of political and civil rights—will seek laws and public actions restricting man's sexual life so that, having established a pattern, they can pursue through public actions and laws social structures that restrict man's more fundamental rights. Therefore, apparently innocuous forms of censorship sometimes have to be vigorously and vigilantly resisted because they are the nose of the totalitarian camel.

We should not assume that people who oppose the censorship of what we may call obscene do so because they are sexual libertines or because they want other people to be sexual libertines. It may be that they are genuinely concerned to achieve and to preserve for the people the fullest possible political and civil freedom, that what they really want is a social habitat in which true morality will be a possibility. For these reasons, then, we will examine the moral significance of censorship apart from any preoccupation with sexual obscenity, although occasionally we shall have to bring the two words together again.

It is important that we give the word "censorship" as much firmness and exactness as possible. In a book titled *Comstockery in America—Patterns of Censorship and Control* (Beacon Press, 1960, pp. 6-7), Robert W. Haney made a helpful distinction and provided a definition. He said:

Thus *censorship* is practiced only by someone, or some group, possessing the authority to back its judgment with legal sanctions or physical compulsion. *Control* is practiced by those who lack such authority but use persuasion to restrict freedom of speech or of the press. . . . Censorship, then, is (1) the imposition of legal restraints upon the production, publication, sale or distribution of any book, pamphlet, magazine, newspaper, photograph, or art object, in order to make it unavailable to most people; (2) the imposition of such restraints upon the production or performance of any public entertainment, including plays, motion pictures, radio broadcasts, or television programs, save for such restraints as may be necessary for the physical safety of the audience (fire law, etc.); and (3) a threat to impose any of the above restraints. Control is identical, except that it is not enforced by legal means.[1]

We could add to Haney's definition the clarifying statement that the objectives of censorship and control are the same but the means are different. Both want to withhold certain books, journals, movies, television, and radio programs from the general public or from some part of the public. Censorship implies the power to make such restrictions total and effective and to penalize those who evade its prohibitions. Control implies the use of ecclesiastical, academic, parental, or nonlegal public pressures and the use of such penalties as the boycott, public ridicule and the threat of legal action. Specifically, then, censorship is governmental action on the local or national level or ecclesiastical action wherever a church can enforce its restrictions by threats and punishments greatly feared by the people and through powers the state grants it.

The distinction between censorship and control should be drawn even finer, and the following examples can help us do so.

Some months ago the Chicago Art Institute refused to exhibit a prize-wining painting, *Events,* by Leanne Shreves, not because it lacked artistic merit but because it was loaded with phallic symbols. The institute officials did not pass judgment on the propriety of exhibiting the painting elsewhere in the city; they merely exercised their privilege of rejecting the painting for a specific exhibition for which they were responsible. Whether the reasons offered

---

[1]Reprinted by permission of the Beacon Press, copyright © 1960 by Robert W. Haney.

for the rejection were valid or not is irrelevant. I would call such an action control rather than censorship. The painting could have been displayed elsewhere and the people who wanted to see it could do so. However, if the mayor of Chicago or any part of his administration had ruled that the painting could not be shown to any people in Chicago under any circumstances, that action would have been censorship and, in my judgment, a reprehensible form of censorship.

If a mother or father prevents a twelve-year-old child from reading Thomas De Quincey's *Confessions of an English Opium-Eater* the prohibition may or may not be wise, depending on the child. But it would be control, not censorship. But if the city of Boston bans the sale of the book or the United States government excludes it from the mails, the action would be censorship.

If an American university forbids a Communist leader's appearance on campus to speak to a group of students, the ban comes under the heading of control, for the Communist can hire a hall and speak to interested students off campus. Such a ban might not be wise, might indeed do far more harm than good; but it cannot be condemned as censorship as long as the students have the privilege of hearing the speaker elsewhere. But if a city, state, or national government prevents a Communist's speaking anywhere, under any circumstances, that is censorship.

So we can conclude that censorship, as distinct from control, presumes to have absolute power and total coverage.

Let us note next that both censorship and control can be either good or bad. Censorship is an absolutely bad word in some quarters and a totally good one in others. But in fact it can be either good or bad, and so can control. Let us look briefly at a few examples of censorship playing a beneficial role in society without harm to the individual. Even Haney in his strict definition allowed for this possibility when he admitted to his definition the conditional clause, "save for such restraints as may be necessary for the physical safety of the audience (fire law, etc.)." But there are a considerable number of legal restraints on communication that protect something more than man's physical safety. Most people will readily concede, for example, that restrictions imposed by the Food and Drug

Administration law on the advertising and labeling of foods and drugs are necessary and beneficial forms of censorship.

Distributors should not be allowed to put untreated milk in cartons labeled "pasteurized." No drug should be advertised as a sure cure for cancer unless it has been proved clinically to cure cancer. Few people condemn the Securities and Exchange Commission regulations governing all kinds of investments. The S.E.C., for example, does not permit insurance companies to issue prospectuses that craftily misrepresent what their policies will produce for their customers.

Caveat emptor—let the customer beware—may have been a sufficient rule of business when man's social structures were simple and the customer could inspect personally both the product for sale and the process that produced it. But today in our highly complex society, where products originate far from the home of the consumer and are so packaged that they cannot be inspected, it is impossible for the customer to beware. How can he know whether the canned meat he buys is tainted, or the cranberry sauce he eats has a heavy and dangerous residue of arsenic from the spraying of the plants, or that the investment house has deliberately advertised worthless bonds? He must rely on the government for some protection against crafty and unscrupulous merchants. And some of the protection the government provides falls under the head of censorship.

Libel laws restrict what an individual or a journal can say about the character or conduct of a person or an organization—even though what is said may be true. Copyright laws restrain the publishing or broadcasting of literary, artistic, and dramatic materials owned by someone other than the one who uses them. All of these are examples of censorship, censorship that is—for reasons we will note later—beneficial to individuals and society.

Control can also be good as well as bad. Parents have every right to control books and magazines their children read, the motion pictures they see, the radio programs they hear, the television broadcasts they view. As we shall see later it is wise for parents to err on the side of elasticity rather than on the side of rigidity. Moreover, it is essential to the growth of the child that the controls be transferred from the outside of the child to the inside as soon as there is any evidence that the child is able to assume responsibility for himself. Responsible journals must exercise control over the material they publish. They reject hundreds of articles a year, some of which may be excellent in quality but may not in the opinion of the editors serve the best interests of their readers.

It can be laid down as a general rule, however, that censorship and control are more harmful to man than beneficial. When wrongly employed these restraints on man's right to know all that he is capable of knowing threaten his freedom and consequently his possibility of becoming a moral creature. It is here, on the dangers of censorship and control, that our attention must linger; for there exists in this country, as among all peoples, an incessant campaign to limit what the people read, hear, and view. Let us look now at some harmful effects of control.

Take first a case of unwise ecclesiastical control. In 1957, Phyllis Woodruff Sapp wrote a book called *The Long Bridge*. This study book was about Guy Bellamy and his work with Negroes as secretary of Negro work for the Southern Baptist Home Mission Board since 1949. As a result of organized pressure against a book dealing with the racial problem and with a courageous effort to solve it, *The Long Bridge*, scheduled for study in January, 1958, was withdrawn from Baptist Book Stores. The executive board of the Mississippi Baptist Woman's Missionary Union designated an alternate book for study, saying that the time was not ripe for a book about Negro work. (This, mind you, was in 1958.) Was this bad control? The Southern Baptist Convention eventually concluded that it was.

In an article titled "It Happened to One Book," published in the April 9, 1958, issue of *The Christian Century*, the author took her case to the churches of the nation and to the general membership of the Southern Baptist Convention. The book was again released to Baptist Book Stores—four months after it had been banned and a few days after the study period was over. Moreover, the author was invited to speak about *The Long Bridge* at the Southern Baptist Convention at Houston, Texas, in May of the same year. As she wrote in *The Christian Century*, "The people had spoken and their voice was heard."

The churches, more than any other nongovernmental institution, have tried to dictate man's knowledge and restrict his sources of knowledge. The Roman Catholic Church, the chief offender, is just now emerging from long centuries of darkness in which it controlled outright in some countries and tried to control in others the people's access to knowledge through any form of communication.

It was only last year that Alfredo Cardinal Ottaviani told the Vatican City weekly newspaper, *L'Osservatore della Domenica,* that the Roman Catholic Index of Forbidden Books has become a "historic document" rather than an applicable and enforceable instrument of censorship. For centuries this list, enforced by threats of excommunication, presumably cut intelligent Roman Catholics off from classical literature, political theory and propaganda, and from scientific studies. Most Protestant churches have been far less rigid and thorough in their thought-control programs. Yet these churches, too, have assumed that the way to make people good is to keep them ignorant.

Almost without exception the churches have been wrong in their censorship and control, and they have been wrong not only in restricting human freedom but in their evaluations of what knowledge is valid, useful, and beneficial to man. Over the years the churches, with occasional exceptions, have taken wrong positions on new theories of the cosmos, the continuing process of creation, the justification of war and slavery, the inerrancy of the Bible. They have not only tried to keep the people from discovering the truth for themselves but have insisted that the people accept and profess error. Every time the church tries to separate the people from what it considers an area of dangerous knowledge, or has tried to brainwash the people, it has championed error rather than truth. On the basis of the churches' records in these areas, and half in jest, it could be said that the one thing the churches should not meddle with is the people's morality.

As far as their official positions are concerned, the churches in the United States today are probably the least dangerous of the organizations dedicated to the control of knowledge and thought. There are in this country numerous would-be censors of American life that must settle for nonlegal methods of imposing their will on the public. The organizations adopt genteel, patriotic, religious names and often operate through conventional civic, social, and religious groups. Unable to use the law in controlling American thought and mores, they resort to boycotts, pickets, letter-writing campaigns, harassing telephone calls, threats of litigation against publishers and merchants and the slandering of public figures with whom they disagree. Their initial attack is against sexual obscenity, but as they succeed their definition of obscenity begins to include radical political ideas, unconventional social theories, the ecumenical movement in the churches, and the struggle for racial justice. They want to silence not only obscenity but also all new, radical, unconventional ideas.

Who are the people who support these vigilante organizations? What are their motives? What do their arrogant attempts to monitor American morality say about *them*? There are three overlapping types of people in the organizations that presume to tell the whole nation what it should not read, hear, or see. Undoubtedly some of these people are utterly conscientious in their belief that they know what is best and safest for the people. They are simple folk, deeply religious and genuinely concerned about the moral quality of the nation. But their definitions of morality are shallow and legalistic; their models of morality are drawn from the pastoral scenes of their childhood; their knowledge of the world is circumscribed by limited experience; their understanding of the paradoxical quality of life and the ambiguities of human nature is inadequate. To such good, simple-minded people all things are either black or white, good or evil, right or wrong; and they see no reason why "what everyone knows is bad" should not be prohibited by law if possible and if not by public pressure. They deeply regret the fact that God in his wisdom—or in a momentary lapse of omniscience—made man capable of sin, and they want to do everything in their power to relieve man of that capability. In the main, such people are found in the churches, especially in those churches that have not undertaken the difficult task of teaching the difference between Christian morality and "piosity"—if I may add a word to *Webster's Unabridged.* These are the people who are vulnerable to manipulation by those who want to control public thought for political purposes.

The second group of people who want the public mind standardized according to their notions of moral and immoral communications must in all kindness be labeled "sick." They have serious mental and emotional twists. They are morbidly afraid of strange ideas and alien customs. Confronted by the new and the different, they feel threatened; they panic; they repulse the imagined danger to themselves by trying to create a society in which they will not be imperiled by the unknown and the unusual.

I see no other explanation but morbidity for the woman who wanted *Robin Hood* removed from the public library because Robin Hood stole from the rich and gave to the poor and therefore had to be a Communist. How else do we explain the local committee of private citizens that tried to remove one of the *Tarzan* series from the library because Tarzan and Jane lived together without benefit of clergy? Research proved that they had been married in a 1915 book before living together. We have to presume "sick" the thousands of Americans who objected to the sale of Garth Williams' book for children, *The Rabbits' Wedding*, because it dealt with the marriage of two rabbits, one black and the other white. They interpreted this innocuous little book as propaganda for interracial marriages.

Sometimes the morbid vigilantes act as they do because they are afraid of themselves or because of personal moods and impulses and unsuspected drives that they do not understand and cannot manage. Like the pathological murderer who begs the police to lock him up so that he will not kill any more people, the morbid redesigners of society want themselves locked away from temptations that might be overpowering.

Anthony Comstock, whose name became a euphemism for censorship in this country, is sometimes cited as a classic example of such projection. No man tried harder and succeeded better in harnessing and checking the American people's right to read what they wanted to read than did Comstock. Yet his biographers say that he had a morbid, relentless sense of his own sin. Certainly it can be surmised that no man in American history spent more of his waking hours—and probably his sleeping ones too—thinking about man's "sinful sexuality" than did Anthony Comstock, the man who devoted his adult life to keeping people from thinking about sex.

The manipulation of people by appealing to their fears, anxieties, and hopes can be a lucrative business. What we generally call the radical right or the extreme right wing in America spends an estimated minimum of fourteen million dollars a year in attacks on the nation's democratic processes.

In their book *Danger on the Right* (Random House, 1964), Arnold Forster and Benjamin R. Epstein wrote: "These Radical Rightists, all too often aided by their conservative allies, pose a threat to our democratic institutions. They undermine confidence in the integrity and patriotism of our elected leaders, our judicial system, our military leaders, our educators, our clergy, our labor leaders—from Washington all the way out to the smallest community in the country. They attack the integrity and patriotism of local officials, clergymen, teachers, and librarians."

One of the primary objectives of these bigoted and autocratic groups is to close the American mind to knowledge and truth by flooding the country with erroneous propaganda and with false charges against American institutions and individuals while at the same time pressuring libraries, colleges, universities, and public schools to ban books and magazines they have condemned. These organizations, large and small, can be numbered in the hundreds and their combined enterprises are a multimillion-dollar operation. We can expect therefore that many of these groups will be headed by charlatans, by men solely concerned about the power they achieve and the profit they gain by appealing to men's hatred, fear, and prejudice.

If it seems that our attention has thus far been concentrated too heavily on the various social and commercial pressures employed to limit communication, this focus has its warranty in the probability that in the United States private pressure is today a greater threat to the free flow of knowledge and ideas than is governmental censorship. But censorship, nevertheless, is perilous to a people in a way that control is not; for censorship—as we have defined it—is a legally sanctioned and enforceable restriction of knowledge and ideas.

Censorship has the weight and power of the government behind it and can employ the various instruments of restraint and punishment available to the state. The power of a dictatorial state to search and seize as it pleases; to withdraw postal privileges; to withhold licenses to publish, broadcast, and stage; to ban public gatherings and to penalize offenders gives governmental censorship a lethal effect that civilian control cannot have.

The history of censorship in the United States at the national level has so many twisted and interlaced strands that we cannot unravel it here. Three general comments are possible and appropriate at this point.

First, the history of censorship in the United States has followed the pattern common in other parts of the world. In most countries censorship arises, first, as an attempt to suppress heretical religious ideas; second, as a way of handling unconventional political ideas; third, as an effort to repress supposedly obscene ideas regarding man's nature as an emotional and sexual being. These periods, of course, are usually overlapping rather than separate. The United States is at the present time clearly in the third of these periods. Public pressure against the expression of certain religious and political ideas remains and is effective. But these ideas and their dissemination are not in general prohibited by federal law.

In regard to religious ideas, the United States Supreme Court has in general followed in recent years the opinion expressed by former Associate Justice Thomas Campbell Clark, who in the *Burstyn* vs. *Wilson* case said: "In seeking to apply the broad and all-inclusive definition of 'sacrilegious' given by the New York courts, the censor is set adrift upon a boundless sea amid a myriad of conflicting currents of religious views, with no charts but those provided by the most vocal and powerful orthodoxies."

These waters, Clark was saying, are too treacherous for the United States government to sail in, and the government should therefore withhold itself from any attempt to regulate the dissemination of religious ideas as such.

Although the high court has been less tolerant of radical political thought, in this area, too, it has moved *toward* rather than *away from* a defense of the people's right to express and to entertain unconventional ideas. So, in the main, federal censorship in the United States has to do with obscenity, as we shall see later.

Therefore we can say, second, that the United States moves more and more toward an open society in which the suppression of information of all kinds will be minimal. This direction has been set by the United States Supreme Court in a series of decisions that in the main have defended man's right to know and to exchange ideas.

Censorship in the United States now is much less general and severe than in the past and far less so than it is in the Soviet Union, Spain, and other totalitarian countries. But we should also note that the sharing of knowledge and ideas is not as free in the United States as it is in the Scandinavian countries and Great Britian.

The "land of the free" is not the land of the freest. On a number of occasions I have sensed in England an air much freer of moral, religious, and political control and censorship than that we breathe in most parts of the United States. (My British friends say that this is a correct judgment as far as political and religious taboos are concerned but that England is just as puritanical about sexual subjects as is the United States.) There will be differences of opinion as to whether this condition is good for the people or bad, but the condition itself is hardly debatable.

Third, we can identify some of the threats of repressive censorship in the United States. At the national level the chief threat to the people's right to know has its seat in the refusal of the Federal Government to keep the people fully informed of the nature, scope, and purpose of this nation's international commitments. Even when it is granted that there are diplomatic maneuvers that should not be prematurely disclosed and military strategies that should not be revealed, there remains a vast area of foreign relations about which the people have the right to be fully informed. In the end they pay the costs of tragic international blunders with their money and their blood. They pay the taxes and fight the wars. They have the right to ask why and to be answered truthfully. But they do not ask why with the vigor and insistence that they should. On the contrary, most Americans supinely conclude that their right to know ends at the water's edge or outside the walls of the Pentagon or just short of the policy-making machinations of the Central Intelligence Agency.

The people do not know what our government is up to in Southeast Asia, the Middle East, and the Caribbean. And when the Administration explains, a credibility gap develops, for the people have good reason to suspect that they are not told the truth. The suppression of information about United States foreign policy and the withholding of the truth about United States involvement in the internal affairs of other nations are probably the most dangerous forms of censorship in this country today.

The censorship of books, magazines, plays, and motion pictures occurs in the United States chiefly at the local or municipal level. Numerous large cities and small towns throughout the country have official and semiofficial committees authorized by the local government to inspect, approve, or ban works of art, literature, and entertainment according to their own standards of acceptability. Frequently the members of these committees are patently incapable of judging the social value, the psychological effect, and the religious significance of the works they ban. Until recently, for example, the official censorship committee in Chicago, Illinois, was composed entirely of women wholly inadequate in education and social sensitivity to determine what the people should read, hear, and view.

Also in Chicago, still the capital of gangsterism in America, a jury convicted a bookseller for selling the book *Fanny Hill.* Later it was discovered that eleven members of the jury had read no books at all during the previous year. So, ironically and tragically, a group of Chicagoans who do not read books had the power to decide what books other Chicagoans could read. It can be laid down as a general rule that those people least competent to test the worth and the potential harm of literature, art, and entertainment are the most willing to impose their standards on the community.

The censorship imposed by local censors often directly and wilfully violates Supreme Court interpretations of the United States Constitution, but appeals to the high court or to lower courts require more time and money than the average merchant or distributor can afford. Consequently, the censor's ruling often goes unchallenged at the local level.

If it is true that freedom is morality's indispensable habitat, that only free men can be genuine persons, then censorship—the suppression of man's freedom to know and to express himself—has an effect exactly opposite to what many conscientious people suppose. For the general assumption is that censorship protects men by isolating them from evil ideas and dangerous knowledge; that it makes them loyal citizens by excluding from their minds all radical political concepts; that it makes them religious and moral by shielding them against exposure to things sacrilegious and obscene. This assumption rests on an erroneous understanding of the nature of man and an inadequate understanding of the meaning of morality. We have mentioned some exceptions, but in general the suppression of the free flow of knowledge and ideas makes men ignorant, servile, obedient; but it does not make them men. On the contrary, to the extent that censorship robs men of their freedom, to that extent it precludes the possibility of their being loyal citizens or genuinely religious and moral men. Censorship, we must conclude, is hostile to authentic morality wherever it limits man's freedom, wherever it narrows the range of his individual decision and personal choice, wherever it constricts his access to any knowledge and any ideas. And censorship is friendly to authentic morality only when it protects man's physical safety and his right to know both truth and error. It was by this principle that we endorsed such censorships as those enforced by the Food and Drug Administration, the Securities and Exchange Commission, libel and copyright laws. These censorships protect man's freedom by guaranteeing him access to the truth. They are indeed the exceptions that prove the rule that censorship in general is hostile to the free spirit of man and detrimental to authentic morality.

This should be the governing perspective from which all people genuinely concerned about man's morality evaluate all censorship: does it liberate man so that he can become fully man or does it imprison and compress his mind and spirit? Our approach to this problem in the past has been entirely wrong, for we have in a variety of ways asked how much freedom we can afford to let the people have when we should have been asking whether, and if so how much, we can afford to limit the people's freedom to read, to hear, and to see without destroying them as persons.

Remember that we are thinking at this point not of private and voluntary controls or of personal discipline but of legally enforceable censorship, of governmental regulation of what passes through the mail and the media. The general rule in this area supports the need for a maximum of personal freedom and a minimum of governmental suppression. The burden of the proof in any debate between those who want man to have a maximum of freedom and those who want his access to ideas restricted should fall always on those who want to censor rather than on those who do not want knowledge and ideas censored. Freedom to receive and to utter ideas should not have to defend itself; censorship should. Freedom is always primary and privileged. Censorship should always be suspect.

Censorship is one of those exasperatingly complex and elusive subjects that vex the mind so much that those who think about it are tempted to plunge toward one extreme or the other. I believe that we should start from the position I have defined—the position that stresses the primacy of freedom—and remain as close to it as possible. But I know also that we become irresponsible if in this matter we become absolutists and allow the government to make no discriminations whatever between what should and should not be censored.

Every man who attempts to draw the line, marking what the government should and should not censor, will immediately appear ridiculous to some other man. But I must run that risk and make three suggestions about the privilege and range of governmental censorship.

First, there is a basic difference between the innate freedom of adults and that of children. I have considerable sympathy for the position taken by Elmer Gertz, a Chicago lawyer long interested in civil rights and censorship cases. In the July 5, 1965, issue of *The Nation,* Gertz explained his progress toward the view that there should be no limitation on adult reading. He concluded: "There must be an end to all censorship of books for adults." I share his belief that "the world will survive with free utterance; it will die when the human mind is fettered in any way." Even so, these are not necessarily the only alternatives, and it is possible to think of books that might endanger human safety and threaten man's free spirit. For example, consider the possible effects of distributing to juveniles throughout the country a do-it-yourself abortion handbook, a manual of instructions for robbing a bank, a code book for the importation of heroin, an illustrated volume on sexual perversions.

I recognize the difficulty of drawing a line between what should and should not pass through the mails. But this does not mean that lines should never be drawn by the government to protect the nation's children.

Even Gertz, who speaks of himself as an absolutist in demanding an end to censorship, makes this distinction between the total freedom to read he would grant all adults and the limited freedom to read he would grant to juveniles. When he says, "I now believe that adults should be permitted to read anything, literally anything," many of us agree. Why should a group of adults in a supposedly free society have the power to determine what other adults can read and cannot read? But state and society correctly assume that there is a fundamental difference between the freedom that is the innate right of adults and the protection that is the inherent right of children. Literature that the average adult can handle, might be deeply and permanently disturbing to an average child with his lack of experience and immature judgment.

A part of the argument about the censoring of adult reading would no doubt end if there were guarantees that books intended solely for adults would not fall into the hands of children. But only a part of the argument would end, for there are people who believe that the government should treat all adults as though they were children. But surely it does not follow that the government should ban the publication and distribution of all books that could in any way be harmful to children. A society that permits its literature to be reduced to that level proves that it *is* juvenile and that it deserves what it gets.

The problem, then, is to protect the right of the adult to read whatever he wants to read without subjecting the child in his formative years to literature that might have a traumatic effect on his developing life. There is no simple rule that cuts through the complexity of this problem, no easy and infallible solution. Certainly it is not wise to turn over the problem of juvenile vulnerability to adult reading, either to the craven extremists who want to ban everything or to the reckless absolutists who would censor nothing.

There will always be a dangerous tension between the freedom to read which is due adults and the need of immature children to be protected from literature that might prevent their becoming real persons. The handling of that tension is, in descending order, the duty of the home, the church, the school and, far down the line, the state. All of these groups should be particularly suspicious of those people who are unwilling to leave the question of good literature or bad to individual judgment but who at the same time want to impose their individual judgment on the whole community. And the whole society should be constantly alert to the possibility that the state will offer its concern for the welfare of children as an excuse for restricting adults.

Furthermore, we should not underestimate the capacity of the average child to handle knowledge about the human body, its functions, and the varieties of human relations. The average child is far more capable of accepting life as it is than most parents and grandparents are willing to grant.

Theoretically, no distinction should be made between the regulations local and federal laws apply to what is portrayed on the stage, in clubs, in movies, and on television. But I would draw a second line and say that there are solid and valid reasons for such discrimination. We will deal later with the probability that we are concerned about and suppress the wrong content on television. For the moment we can say that the greater the medium's exposure to juveniles, the more justified we are in controlling and censoring what it portrays. As with literature, so here the distinction rests on the difference between the maturity and responsibility of the average adult and the mental and emotional immaturity of the average child. (Note that we have said "the average adult" and "the average child," for governmental censorship can be concerned only about the average person, not about the exceptional one.)

The distinction we need to make is not between art forms and entertainment media as such but the accessibility of their presentations to children. I, for one, would allow almost boundless latitude to the theater in the presentation of sacrilege, political radicalism, and sexual obscenity. In fact, we do so every time we allow the staging of Shakespeare's *Hamlet*—a play that portrays murder, incestuous thoughts, allusions to fornication, political treachery, and that is liberally sprinkled with "dirty words" in their King James version. To ban *Hamlet* for any of these reasons from any of the media would rob man of a most valuable possession. But to translate *Hamlet* into terms easily understood by immature children and to broadcast this version of violence and sexual aberration over television during the hours when young children are among the viewers would be a betrayal of our duty to our children.

Third, in trying to make limited censorship creative rather than destructive, I would distinguish between the great latitude that a healthy society should allow the serious artist and the more restricted freedom that it should allow the commercial entertainer. I grant the difficulty in many instances of separating the one from the other, but the difficulty is not insuperable.

The intent of the serious artist who wants to mirror all of life and its possibilities faithfully is in most cases obviously different from that of the commercial entertainer who merely wants to make money, and who is contemptuous of all personal and social values. The United States Supreme Court has made this criterion one of its touchstones.

The court insists—as it did when, in 1966, it overturned a Massachusetts banning of John Cleland's *Fanny Hill*, that a work must not be barred from the public unless it be wholly lacking in redeeming social value. The serious artist in every field is concerned about personal and/or social values; but the purely commercial entertainer, scornful of all values save the monetary one, will appeal to what is basest in man—hatred, bigotry, fear, and lust—to increase his profit.

To make my point plain, I should say that the commercial entertainer should be put under the least possible restraint consistent with adult freedom and the protection of children, and that serious artists should be granted a latitude beyond that allowed mere entertainers.

It also follows from this principle that there should be no censorship of serious studies of man as a religious, political, and sexual creature, however shocking the revelations of these studies may be. We may not be pleased, for example, by the Kinsey reports of sexual behavior in the human male and the human female. These reports, of course, are not infallible. But they are serious attempts to record how man's behavior as a sexual creature actually looks when the façades are stripped away and he is exposed as he really is. Increased knowledge leads to increased understanding, which in turn leads to increased freedom. Freedom does not produce authentic morality, but without it there can be no genuine morality.

We have now seen that the control and the censorship of human communication are highly questionable, potentially dangerous, and occasionally necessary human enterprises. The control and censorship of knowledge, ideas, and feelings—though required under certain circumstances—must be viewed generally as hostile to that human freedom that is indispensable to authentic morality. Under all circumstances, the question to be raised is not how much freedom we can afford to trust to people but whether we can afford to let some people restrict the right of other adults to read, hear, and view what they please. We have acknowledged that young children's lack of experience and mature judgment and their vulnerability to some knowledge and ideas that can be handled by the average adult place them in their early years in a category of human need requiring a wise control and censorship of the media to which they are exposed. But throughout these words there has run a constant stress on man's right to know and to think and to share with other men what he knows and thinks. For to the degree that he is deprived of this right, to that degree he ceases being and becoming fully man.

5
Obscenity Beyond Sex

If it is helpful to separate censorship from obscenity in order to see it clearly, it is even more important to examine obscenity apart from censorship. Both of these concepts are hard to grasp but of the two obscenity is by far the more slippery and elusive. What is obscenity and what is obscene? For several years now the United States Supreme Court has been trying to answer these apparently simple questions. Yet the highest judicial body in this country, composed of some of the nation's wisest minds, has failed to define to its own satisfaction, or to that of anyone else, a commonly used word that the great majority of Americans throws around positively and with much confidence. This fact should be sufficient to make the people enter this field with great caution, but unfortunately it is not.

For as long as it could the Supreme Court avoided coming to grips with this thorny subject, but eventually it had to do so. In 1957 the court laid down in the *Roth* vs. *United States* case a definition of obscenity that for several years was the classical and legal test. The Roth decision stated that the test of obscenity rests on "whether to the average persons, applying contemporary community standards, the dominant theme of the material taken as a whole appeals to prurient interest."

Judge Clayton Horn of California, who presided over the "Howl" and Lenny Bruce trials, applied this test when he defined obscenity as follows: "Obscenity means, to the average person, applying contemporary standards, the predominant appeal of the matter, taken as a whole, to prurient interest, that is a shameful or morbid interest in nudity, sex, or excretion, which goes substantially beyond customary limits of candor in description or representation of such matters and in matter which is utterly without redeeming social importance." In this definition there are at least nine elastic words that cannot themselves be precisely defined: obscenity, average, contemporary, predominant, prurient, shameful, morbid, substantially, and customary. These words are all general, relative, or subjective. They either cover great territory or evoke personal opinion and individual taste.

When the courts began using the word "prurient," the public thought that here at last was an infallible formula for deciding between the clean and the unclean. To be prurient is to have an itchy, lustful interest—in this case in the sexual—or, as Judge Horn put it, "a shameful or morbid interest in nudity, sex, or excretion." But who can say unequivocally that an individual's sexual arousal is lustful rather than wholesome, morbid rather than healthy, except in extreme cases? How tempting it is for any one of us to conclude that his sexual interests are natural but that the other person's are lustful and depraved.

To an unmarried female associate with whom I worked many years ago, and who in every other respect was a quite sensible woman, every man who surveyed a woman's body with appreciation was "a sex maniac"—a judgment that, obviously, would find every man guilty of prurience. So—I am suggesting—the Supreme Court and the lower courts got off to a bad start in their attempts to pin down obscenity. They tried to give the word substance by modifying it with vague, general, subjective adjectives—an obviously ineffective approach to a probably impossible task.

Nearly ten years after the *Roth* vs. *United States* case, the United States Supreme Court issued on March 21, 1966, three decisions that made the waters of obscenity even murkier than they had been. First, the Supreme Court upheld by a 5 to 4 vote the obscenity conviction of Ralph Ginzburg, publisher of *Eros* and other erotic literature. In this case the court ruled that the situation as well as the material, and especially the manner in which he promoted the sale of his material, had to be taken into account. It held that a piece of material which might not in itself be obscene could become obscene because of "the context of the circumstances of production, sale, and publicity." It appears, indeed, that Ginzburg did everything he could to challenge the Roth decision, to irritate the court, and to draw from it a prejudiced and unstable decision. Whether that was his intention or not, that is what he accomplished; and he may have to spend five years in the federal penitentiary for his success.

The Ginzburg decision seemed so strange to us that *The Christian Century* editors made the following comment in an April 13, 1966, editorial:

> The introduction of advertising and promotion as factors in the testing of obscenity clouds rather than clarifies the problem; for by this test the Bible, a Sears, Roebuck catalogue and *Little Women* could be made obscene even though not obscene per se. Few people will quarrel with the argument that advertising and promotion can in themselves be pornographic, but that they confer obscenity on a particular piece of material is an unwarranted conclusion. Justice Douglas correctly pointed out in his dissent that "sexy advertisement neither adds to nor detracts from the quality of the merchandise being offered for sale. And I do not see how it adds or detracts one whit from the legality of the book being distributed. A book should stand on its own, irrespective of the reasons why it was written or the wiles used in selling it. Whatever the other demerits or merits of this decision it is unlikely that this aspect of the Ginzburg decision will survive rethinking by the justices."

The Supreme Court's second 1966 decision on obscenity upheld the conviction of Edward Mishkin of Yonkers, New York, for selling materials which the publisher—Mishkin—admitted to be "sadistic and masochistic." However, it was the court's ruling in the third case that made its Ginzburg decision seem ridiculous. A Massachusetts court had ruled that *Fanny Hill*—John Cleland's 1750 *Memoirs of a Woman of Pleasure*—"is not entitled to the protection of the First and Fourteenth Amendments to the Constitution of the United States." The Supreme Court held that *Fanny Hill* passes the Roth test, that it does not as a whole appeal to prurient interest in sex, offend contemporary community standards, and wholly lack redeeming social significance. I do not subscribe to the Roth test of obscenity, but if it is used I do not see how *Fanny Hill* escaped the court's condemnation. It may have social value, but not *redeeming* social value. And if this endless and therefore boring recitation of a London prostitute's escapades does not stimulate lustful interest in sex it was certainly intended to do so. Indeed, the author's concentration on male genitals and sexual prowess in a book designed for male consumption suggests the probability that the author was expressing and seeking to arouse homosexual interests.

Here, then, in two decisions in the same session the court condemned a man for obscene advertising and promotion of erotic literature yet passed favorably on the sale of a book that deals solely with the life of a whore. I am not suggesting that these decisions should have been reversed but rather that they are logically and legally incompatible.

We expressed our editorial astonishment over the confusion of the court in *The Christian Century* to which I have already referred in the following words that sought some explanation of the court's dilemma:

> The thorny side of this issue has its origin in the increasing number of Americans who find wanton public descriptions of man's sexual nature and behavior repugnant and dangerous and who demand that the courts legally restrict such expressions. Many Americans have watched with understandable alarm the increasing torrents of pornography flooding newsstands, drug stores, candy and tobacco shops, and the mails. They are angered by the ease with which young people in major cities can purchase photographs which depict male and female genitals in exaggerated and titillating postures and magazines and books which describe in minute and lurid detail every form of hetero- and homosexual aberration and which encourage the expression of latent sadism and masochism in sexual relations. No doubt this rebellion is in some cases motivated by prudery and by neurotic views of man's sexual life, but to dismiss the revolt against libertinism in public expression as nothing more than this would be a grievous mistake. Many responsible, intelligent and sophisticated people are genuinely disturbed by what appears to them an inordinate public craving for lewdness, by the increasing number of panderers who for selfish purposes cultivate this craving and by the panderers' concentration of their sales campaign on youth. Moreover, some of the objectors are wise

enough to see that erotic pictures and literature, rather than being aphrodisiac, are actually sexual sedatives which substitute for and lessen the capacity for normal sexual love.

But when the justices grasp this side of the issue of obscenity—as in two of these cases they tried to do—their judicial responsibility is pricked by another and more serious issue: the right of free speech and expression and the right of the people to every kind of information. In the Ginzburg case four of the justices—Douglas, Black, Harlan and Stewart—found the competing issue so paramount that they could not concur in the majority opinion. Since Justices Black and Douglas are categorically opposed to all forms of censorship, Stewart's dissenting opinion may be more enlightening. In part he said: "Censorship reflects a society's lack of confidence in itself. It is a hallmark of an authoritarian regime. Long ago those who wrote our First Amendment charted a different course. They believed a society can be truly strong only when it is truly free. In the realm of expression they put their faith, for better or for worse, in the enlightened choice of the people, free from the interference of a policeman's intrusive thumb or a judge's heavy hand. So it is that the Constitution protects coarse expression as well as refined and vulgarity no less than elegance."

To the extent that the national mood is preoccupied with lasciviousness and perversion in all forms of public media we have a problem, but that problem cannot be corrected by the enactment of a law—certainly not by a bad law. And if the Supreme Court empowers federal censorship we invite into the national body demons far more perilous than sexual wantonness. The difficulty is to correct the one problem—admittedly grave—without generating a host of others.

The slippery side of the issue has its origin in our proved inability to define the word "obscenity." To be sure, there are many people who cannot spell the word but who are positive that they can define what is and what is not obscene. They know. But nine of the wisest men in the United States do not know. The ignorance of the latter is much more to be trusted than the arrogance of the former. A pound or a meter or a boiling point can be precisely defined, but obscenity lies in a wholly different realm and has thus far resisted definition. In the Ginzburg and Mishkin cases the majorities of the court ignored what they know they do not know: they did not have and they will not have an inflexible standard by which to test obscenity. Therefore the court in its three split decisions conceived arbitrary lines of legitimate literary traffic and painted those lines on the shifting sands of "contemporary community standards," the motivations of publishers, "the leer of the sensualist"—strange language for a justice—"redeeming social value," obscenity by context. Subjective analysis, the probing of people's motives, the sampling of public taste—these are not solid foundations on which to erect the nation's laws. The court will be back at this stand again and, we predict, soon. In these cases the court started something, ended nothing.

Our prediction that the court would soon take up this issue again in an effort to undo the confusion sown by its 1966 decisions was fulfilled sooner than we had expected. In an unsigned 7 to 2 ruling in May, 1967, the court issued a ruling permitting the sale of a long list of "girlie" magazines without recrimination to either the seller or the publisher. In a four-page decision the court permitted the sale of certain sex-oriented paperbacks and such magazines as *Bachelor, Modern, Man, Gent, Swank, Cavalcade, Sir, Ace, Spree,* and *High Heels.* This decision indicates that the Supreme Court is uneasy about its Ginzburg decision. Two of the dissenting justices in the 1967 obscenity ruling—John M. Harlan and Tom C. Clark—said that this action "does not reflect well on the processes of the court." So, nine of the wisest men in the country, having boundless resources and a large corps of competent advisers, leave us still asking the question, "What is obscenity?"

It is well known that words experience continuous metamorphosis, that they sometimes accumulate a variety of meanings and at other times become narrowly focused, that they can even in a few swift years reverse their meaning. The word "obscenity" has had that kind of history. In the beginning, the Latin word *obscenus* meant inauspicious, ill-omened, a bad sign. Later it came to mean filthy, abominable, indecent. *Webster's New Collegiate Dictionary* defines the obscene as "1. disgusting to the senses; repulsive. 2. abhorrent to morality or virtue; specifically, designed to incite to lust or depravity." In common usage today the word has an exclusively sexual connotation. We can define the word, but I suggest that it is impossible to know precisely what it is that the word names.

We have seen that thus far the Supreme Court has found it impossible to define criminal obscenity. I suggest that it is for the same reason equally impossible to define cultural and religious obscenity. The reason for this inability, as I have already indicated, is very simple. Obscenity is a matter of personal opinion and individual taste—two human attributes that have a wide latitude of varieties.

In a June 16, 1965, article in *The Christian Century,* Robert Tracy, assistant professor of English at the University of California in Berkeley, illustrated the absurdities that result from attempts to treat obscenity as though it were a definite substance. He wrote: "The word [obscenity] is open-ended, subjective—a situation at present exemplified in California where Genêt's film *Chant d'amour* is obscene in Alameda County but not obscene across the bay in San Francisco. The word 'obscene' changes meaning exactly in the middle of the bay bridge, at the county line, and every writer knows that when words are made to behave in this chameleonic fashion communication is impossible."

Obscenity, then, is relative. A humorous story has it that a fundamentalist college in the South expelled one of the women students for indecent exposure—she had a hole in the knee of her bathing suit. I learned when I was in New Delhi, India, that it is considered indecent for a young man and a young woman to walk the streets hand in hand or arm in arm but that young men who show each other such endearments on the street are not considered indecent or queer.

In the work I have quoted, Robert W. Haney said that "to a Chinese gentleman, the 'Stars and Stripes Forever' may be disgustingly lascivious. An Arab considered doughnut-dunking an exceedingly lewd practice. The exposure of the face of a Moslem woman was at one time deemed an impure act, and no Eskimo woman can be regarded as virtuous who removes her boots in the presence of strange men."

When I was a boy in the rural South a mother who nursed her baby in public was not considered obscene. Today the same natural act is considered indecent. Five years ago only prostitutes would have appeared on city streets—and then only on certain streets—in the mini-skirts many women wear casually—but most men do not view casually—in public places today. The dress that was considered obscene will through familiarity cease seeming indecent and, in fact, will soon cease being an aphrodisiac. These are sufficient illustrations to show that obscenity is relative to custom and is not an absolute.

Since obscenity is relative, it cannot be said that anything is obscene in itself. Rather, everything must be subjected to the test of appropriateness—to Aristotle's rule of proportion. Is it expedient? Does it belong? In our society—to take some examples—men and women do not normally appear naked on the streets. If they do, they are apprehended by the police and, if sane, are usually required to pay a penalty. But a person who flees naked from a burning building would not be thought immoral, insane, nor a violator of public conventions and sensibilities.

Some years ago I saw the graceful and tender statue of *The Sleeping Hermaphrodite* in the National Museum of Rome. This statue's open exhibition to the whole public was entirely appropriate in that setting, but it would be inappropriate in the lobby of a boy's school. I think no great painting ever hit me with quite the staggering blow that Goya's *Saturn Devouring His Children* did in the Prado Gallery in Madrid. This painting is a master work by a master artist, and it should be exhibited, despite the effect it has on squeamish stomachs. But it would be indecent to hang *Saturn Devouring His Children* in a public restaurant. Photographic depictions of the effects of venereal disease would be appropriate at a medical convention but hardly so at a bridal party.

Some of the four-letter words have appeared in *The Christian Century* and, undoubtedly, will appear in the future. When the question has arisen as to whether the offensive word should remain in the text, the question has been answered by the test of appropriateness. Does the ugly word belong? Is it integral to what the writer is trying to say? Or, is the author merely a little boy trying to write an insignificant but shocking word on a wall?

The Bible, of course, is the superb literary example of the redemptive character of expediency and appropriateness. Almost every form of sexual activity known to man—including masturbation, fornication, adultery, homosexuality, sodomy, and sexual intercourse between human beings and animals—is mentioned in the Bible. But few people, as far as I know, have seriously contended that these passages should be taken out of the Bible or that the Bible should be taken out of the hands of children. You cannot describe man without describing aberrant and sinful man. But a film made from excerpts of the Bible's numerous sexual references and broadcast over television for general consumption would be indecent.

The same principle applies when we are considering whether a specific piece of literature, drama, or art is obscene. Literature, drama, and art are mirrors held up to man in all his dimensions. As John Henry Cardinal Newman once said, "If literature is to be made a study of human nature, you cannot have a Christian literature. It is a contradiction in terms to attempt a sinless literature of sinful man." If art, drama, and literature are to have any integrity at all, latitude must be permitted for a candid presentation of man as he is. There is no good reason why we should permit the Bible to deal with man's depravity and not permit literature, drama, and art to do so. Indeed, these representations of man greatly enrich our understanding of what the Bible says about him.

To the test of appropriateness, I would add the test of honesty in determining what is and what is not obscene. I have examined hard-core pornography and am acquainted with many of the magazines that skirt the edge of pornography. But I would say that magazines such as *Playboy* are more obscene and more threatening to authentic morality than is much of what we call pornography. This is so, not because of the easy accessibility of *Playboy* and the general acceptability of such magazines in our day, but because the *Playboy* type preaches a fundamentally dishonest doctrine of sex, of womanhood, and of the highest good of life. I am in complete agreement with what Ralph A. Cannon said in an article called "Pornography, Sex and the Church." In *The Christian Century*, May 1, 1963, he wrote:

> The magazine [*Playboy*] still assumes that sex is a plaything with no significance beyond a moment's pleasure. . . . As long as *Playboy* panders to a juvenile fascination with sexual trivia while calling itself sophisticated, it remains a menace to Christian character. . . . It is not primarily the sheer quantity of unadorned flesh and unrefined language in these periodicals that elicits our concern. Rather it is the over-all ideology—the notion that women are playtime toys

for men to dawdle with; that sex is merely a biological function, i... the same category as eating and breathing, and to be indulged at will; that love is just a sentimental impediment, an unnecessary complication; that erotic pleasure is the supreme good in life. It is this ideology that makes these magazines vile.

Playboy, Cannon was saying, is a huge and destructive put-on that deceives men and debases women. This basic dishonesty rather than the retouched portraits of nude women makes it necessary for me to identify *Playboy* and similar magazines as soft-core pornography rather than calling them in the current mode innocuous and sophisticated fun.

The answer to such obscenity is not the banning of such magazines but the freeing of serious books and magazines so that they may deal honestly with the sexual theme in all of its ramifications. In the March, 1961, issue of *Commentary,* Paul Goodman raised a pertinent question: "What if the censorship itself, part of a general repressive antisexuality, causes the evil, creates the need for sadistic pornography sold at criminal profit?" He put his comment in the form of a question, but I believe we can be more positive.

It is possible that a completely liberated literature that can deal with the sexual theme honestly and in all candor will drive pornography out of business and greatly diminish the heavy flow of paperbacks and magazines that debase sex and dishonor women. Father Anthony Schillaci of Chicago, a member of the awards committee for the National Catholic Office for Motion Pictures, believes that this thesis can also be applied to motion pictures. He said recently that the so-called art films which treat sex honestly are greatly to be desired over the entertainment movies that treat sex dishonestly: "The Doris Day will-she-or-won't-she epics are very destructive because they don't treat sex honestly."

Characteristically, we ask the wrong questions about movies and television programs that use sexual material: How much flesh was revealed? Were "dirty words" used? Was the material sexually stimulating?

We should ask whether the material and the manner in which it was presented debase sex, impose on viewers a false philosophy of the nature and purpose of life and corrupt their concept of the worth of human beings. No young person will be corrupted by an exposed breast in a motion picture or by a responsible and truthful description of the sexual factor in human love. But they can be corrupted by an enticingly promoted hedonism that turns women into instruments for the gratification of men, that makes coitus the supreme good, and that cultivates irresponsible human relations.

The line between sexual obscenity and hard-core pornography is wavy and blurred; but in general we can say that hard-core pornography consists of photographs, drawings, movies, or descriptions of people engaged in normal or aberrant forms of sexual intercourse or auto-eroticism. The general public has little, but nevertheless increasing, access to this underworld sexual material. Pornography has no serious intent except to encourage and satisfy strange tastes and to do it for profit. It is sometimes called "dirt for dirt's sake." But as someone has said, it is better called "dirt for money's sake."

It may surprise you, and certainly will interest you, to know that the most searing denunciation of pornography was written by D. H. Lawrence, whose controversial book *Lady Chatterley's Lover* was not cleared for distribution in the United States until 1959. Lawrence's governing purpose in *Lady Chatterley's Lover* was to glorify sexual love; but he was himself an implacable foe of pornography and believed that it should be censored.

I am indebted to Haney for the following quotation from Lawrence's *Selected Literary Criticism* chapter on "Pornography and Obscenity" (Viking, 1955). Lawrence wrote: "Pornography is the attempt to insult sex, to do dirt on it. This is unpardonable. Take the very lowest instance, the picture postcard sold underhand, by the underworld, in most cities. What I have seen of them has been of an ugliness to make you cry. The insult to the human body, the insult to a vital human relationship! Ugly and cheap they make the human nudity, ugly and degraded they make the sexual act, trivial and cheap and nasty."

Intelligent, sophisticated people have denounced *Lady Chatterley's Lover* as obscene because its preoccupation with sexual acts seems an inordinate glorification of the sexual act and because it is a tacit approval of adultery. But the book's concentration on sexual love is probably as much a literary weakness as a moral one. But

Lawrence's controversial book is certainly not pornographic, even if its excesses make it obscene. Lawrence attempted an honest rescue of the sexual life from the gutter and from the men's smoking room. The book has the weaknesses I have mentioned, but it must be said at the same time that it was beautifully and tenderly written. Obscene in its exaltation of sexual love, perhaps, the book is nevertheless *not* pornographic.

If pornography is a defilement of sex and a debasement of the physical expression of romantic love, then our culture is saturated with a corruption of sex far more dangerous than the still-limited sale of filthy pictures, sordid magazines, and stag-party films. We do not notice this soft-core pornography because we swim in it all the time. I am referring to the widespread exploitation of sex in the advertisement of articles ranging from automobiles to toilet paper.

Sex itself does not have to be sold; therefore it is used to sell other things. The advertising industry uses two approaches in this exploitation of sex.

The first is the open appeal to sexual interest: a voluptuous girl squirming on a tiger skin while she purrs lasciviously about the merits of the product she advertises; a seductive blond who transfers to television from burlesque the chant, "Take it off; take it all off," to sell Noxzema shaving cream; customers and clerks in a grocery store receiving ecstatic pleasure as they surreptitiously squeeze rolls of toilet tissue—these are current illustrations of television commercials that make the open sexual pitch.

The second approach is a more subtle use of sexual imagery—even of various phallic symbols—to maintain the viewers' interest and to produce a favorable response to the advertised product.

The danger in this exploitation of sex to sell products not directly related to man's sexual life is not that the viewer will be deceived into buying a Dodge rather than a Ford, or Camels rather than Chesterfields, or beer A rather than beer B. The danger is that the viewer will be deceived into buying the notion that sexual desirability and sexual proficiency are the highest measures of human worth and that sex is the ultimate criterion of all values. Hard-core pornography is a visible enemy with which we can grapple with some success. But the kind of soft-core pornography that appears in television commercials—the sex-exploiting and sex-glorifying advertisements—carries a germ difficult to isolate and eliminate.

It follows that concerned people should concentrate their energies not on the censoring of pornography but on the creation of a climate in which commercials that exploit and inordinately glorify sex will fail to sell products and in which a degree of honesty returns to advertising. Until this occurs television commercials will have a more powerful influence on the nation's folklore of sex than do the churches. While our attention is concentrated on the underworld that produces and distributes hard-core pornography, a soft-core pornography, that debases women as persons, distorts sex either by insulting it or by making it the crown of all human experience, and interprets all of life in hedonistic terms, fills the popular magazines and the airwaves.

Two more correctives are necessary before we turn to some remarks about obscenity beyond sex. First, many devout religious people erroneously and dishonestly denounce as obscene anything that arouses sexual desire. Judge Jerome Frank said in 1949: "No sane man thinks that the arousing of normal sexual desires is socially dangerous." Unfortunately, he was wrong. Many sane people think, or say they think, that the arousing of sexual desires is bad for persons and for society. This is an erroneous conclusion, for it is simply another way of saying that the sexual nature of man is itself evil. Our Puritan forefathers and, before them, many Roman Catholic theologians believed this, altogether forgetting that physically we are what God made us and what he made he called good. It was God and not the devil who made us male and female and planted in us the impulses and instincts that drive men and women toward each other. To call the sexual nature of man evil or to condemn automatically everything that stirs man sexually is to insult the wisdom of the Creator.

The case of James Joyce's *Ulysses* was a watershed in the history of American attitudes toward censorship and obscenity. Judge John M. Woolsey of the United States District Court for southern New York decided in 1933 that the ban against *Ulysses* should be lifted and that the book should be admitted to the United States. This action got the first olive out of the bottle, and the rest then came easier. But in this liberating decision, Judge Woolsey defined obscenity as "tending to stir the sex impulses or to lead to sexually impure and lustful thoughts."

There is, in my opinion, no defense for the stirring of "sexually impure and lustful thoughts," if we can decide what they are. But I see no ground on which the stirring of normal sex impulses can in itself be condemned. The critic who condemns the arousal of man's sexual impulses is usually thinking about the other person's sexuality and not about his own; he is concerned about the other person's becoming sexually depraved and not about himself; he finds the other person's sexual behavior distasteful but not his. He is therefore patently dishonest when he condemns the stirring of sex impulses as obscene.

As a pastor, I encountered a number of situations in which marriages could have been saved and families preserved if the sexual impulses of the wife or the husband could have been aroused and in which the external inducement of aroused sexual interest might have served a good purpose. But—apart from that significant fact—it is dishonest to condemn literature and art that are sexually stimulating and at the same time to participate without protest in a culture saturated with blunt and subtle aphrodisiacs: dress, cosmetics, perfume, music, dancing and—I might add—the moon.

The arousal of sexual impulses is natural; and it is natural that they should be stirred by stimuli external to man as a physical creature as well as by internal pressures. Attempts to impede these natural impulses only guarantee that they will emerge in aberrant and harmful forms. Even the devout celibate must develop some way to discharge his sexual energies or be overpowered by them.

The point I am trying to make was put neatly by Justice Douglas in his dissenting opinion in the *Roth* vs. *United States* Supreme Court decision. He said: "The tests by which these convictions were obtained require only the arousing of sexual thoughts. Yet the arousing of sexual thoughts and desires happens every day in normal life in dozens of ways. Nearly thirty years ago a questionnaire sent to college and normal school women graduates asked what things were most stimulating sexually. Of 409 replies, 9 said 'music';

18 said 'pictures'; 29 said 'dancing'; 40 said 'drama'; 95 said 'books'; and 218 said 'man.'" The sexual interest can be controlled and re-directed, but it lies close to the surface in most normal human beings. It responds to numerous and varied stimuli. Neither the stimuli nor the response can be categorically condemned as evil.

So there is another kind of obscenity—a dishonest, erroneous, hypocritical antisexuality that rebukes rather than praises God for the way he made man, that views the sexual act as something nasty that has to be tolerated for the propagation of the race, that be-lieves that the enjoyment of this necessity compounds its wicked-ness. If we are correct—and historically we are—in calling this attitude of antisexuality Puritan, then it has to be said that Puri-tanism is also a form of pornography. It debases sexual love, de-spises the sexual factor in man's nature and—the exact opposite of hedonism—condemns physical pleasure as wicked. It does so sin-cerely or hypocritically and in either case is wrong. Moreover, Puritan repressions of sexual impulses tend to drive those impulses toward deviant expressions and tend to produce in those people taught to be ashamed of their sexual life enormous and destructive deposits of guilt. "Dirt for money's sake" is pornographic, but so also is that attitude that views man's sexual nature and his normal sexual activity as dirt.

We shall examine later at some length the relation of law to morality, so we will only mention at this point the second of two necessary correctives of our common view of obscenity. It needs to be said with considerable emphasis that there is no ground for the presumption that all things offensive to our moral, aesthetic, or religious senses should be prohibited by control or by censorship.

When we have agreed that a piece of art, a play, or a book is offensive we have not thereby proved that it should be eliminated. This is so not only because of the obvious dangers of censorship but also because the shocking event or the offensive communication may be the channel through which new truth breaks into our con-sciousness. This does not mean that God always uses the ugly and shocking to speak to us. It merely means that he sometimes does and that if we automatically reject what is offensive to our taste or to our spirit we will sometimes slam the door on that God who comes to us as he pleases. After all, in the day in which Jesus was crucified the cross was an obscene instrument, the most offensive of all instruments of torture and death. Yet it was through this obscenity—a bloody, fly-filthy stake—that God revealed to us his redeeming love.

Sometimes the offense is needed to penetrate solidified minds and hardened hearts. The obscene may be destructive, but it also can be creative. If we automatically exclude everything we dislike, prohibit everything distasteful, we have no chance to discover whether it is the one or the other.

For practical purposes we accepted the dictionary's definition of obscenity: "1. disgusting to the senses; repulsive. 2. abhorrent to morality or virtue; specifically, designed to incite to lust or depravity." If it is true that everything abhorrent to morality or virtue is obscene, is it not strange and is it not revealing that 99 percent of our concern about obscenity focuses on sex?

In an article with the strange title "Pornography Is Not Enough" in the November, 1960, issue of *Harper's,* Eric Larrabee gave a superb illustration of the direction in which these thoughts now move. He wrote: "The time-tested formula for the sexed-up cover of a paperback book is a near-naked girl with a revolver, and it is curious that critics should comment so often on the nudity and ignore the invitation to murder."

Larrabee's position is well taken. We have concentrated the condemnatory word "obscene" on one area of the human experience and have by inference declared that morality and virtue are threatened only by man's abuse of his sexual life.

Why does this happen? Why do we complain about the nude and ignore the revolver? Let me suggest two of the obvious answers to these questions. Sex is an intriguing subject difficult to ignore even by the morbidly prudish. If their inhibitions prevent their discussing sexual matters normally and candidly, censoriousness gives them an opportunity to do so obliquely and negatively.

When I was a youth, a roving, free-lance evangelist pitched his tent one summer in a vacant lot adjacent to our home. We were compelled to listen to his fire-and-brimstone sermons whether we wanted to or not. But, in fact, the sermons were most interesting to this boy in his early teens. For in denouncing the sexual vices of the people the evangelist delivered the most titillating descriptions of sexual activity I had ever heard. Under the guise of a self-righteous condemnation of the sexual lives of other people, the evangelist and his congregation gorged themselves on sexual fantasies. A censorious preoccupation with the sexual behavior of other people is often nothing more than an indulgence of a morbid preoccupation with sex or an attempt to satisfy famished sexual desires. For this reason many people are drawn irresistibly, even though negatively, toward sexual themes.

Second, we criticize nudity or some other supposed sexual obscenity and "ignore the invitation to murder" so that our preoccupation with the first will exempt us from responsibility for the second. We expend ourselves in attacks on sexual obscenity so that we may excuse ourselves for our involvement in the more numerous and grosser obscenities of our culture.

An obsession with personal cleanliness or with social correctness or moralistic properness can be a substitute for social concern and ethical responsibility. The young man who came to Jesus asking about the good life had scrupulously kept the law—an accomplishment Jesus did not deride. But this obsession with the law was the young man's substitute for a life of generosity and charity beyond the law. And he went away sorrowful when Jesus challenged him to accept the fuller life. Likewise an inordinate alarm about sexual obscenity—even though not censorious—can be a decoy, diverting our attention and our concern from the more hideous obscenities in which our lives are submerged and which we accept without protest or alarm.

If obscenity means "abhorrent to morality or virtue," and if authentic morality has to do with the transforming of people into persons, then we should vastly increase the scope of the word "obscenity." For sexual obscenity is only one of the numerous threats to morality. It should not be excluded from our concern, but neither should it be allowed to blind us to the fact that our society is suffused with dangers to true morality worse than any sexual abnormality. These are the threats that we should be most vigorously protesting and resisting.

I am thinking, for example, of the vicious defamation of character that occurs across racial and religious lines: the poisonous jokes that perpetuate erroneous and slanderous stereotypes about Negroes or Jews; the delicious but sickening rumors about men in high places in our national life, rumors about them and their families; the diatribes against the National Council of the Churches of Christ spewed over the country by radio's "apostles of discord." In one week the programs of these extremists spread more vile and deadly obscenity over this country in their relentless accusations against responsible and conscientious churchmen than a dozen "girlie" magazines do in a year.

I know pious and proper Christians whose lips have never been parted by one of the four-letter words but who, with the greatest ease, hurl at human beings the contemptuous and offensive word "nigger." I know other Christians who are horrified by jokes that have sexual connotations but not by those that degrade members of other races, religions, and classes. If a choice must be made, the former are preferable to the latter. Whatever poisons our minds against human beings, dishonors them as persons, or cuts off our communication with them is obscene.

How easily, unconsciously and sometimes innocently, we drift into this kind of obscenity.

Every ten years great masses of Christians from all over the world witness the *Passion Play* at Oberammergau, Germany. For many of them, this pilgrimage is the high point in a lifetime of religious experiences. Yet, as they witness the passion of Christ in the particular script employed at Oberammergau, they are indoctrinated with a venomous anti-Semitism which charges Jews with the heinous crime of deicide.

Following his visit to Oberammergau, in 1960, Tom F. Driver wrote a criticism of the play, in which he stated: "The play *is* decidedly anti-Semitic, and its interpretation of the crucifixion and the events leading to it is harmful not only to Christian-Jewish relations but to proper understanding of the gospel." This is not merely the view of a few hypersensitive American critics. Several members of the cast rebelled against the ancient, anti-Semitic script and campaigned for an updated version of the Passion Week drama that would be faithful to the Scriptures and yet would not defame Jews. They failed. So thousands of Christians will again in 1970 be exposed to the ugliest, most unjust, and untrue charges of anti-Semitism. They will absorb obscenity while they watch a dramatization of that event in which God revealed his perfect love for all men, including Jews!

Such slanders of Jews are "abhorrent to morality or virtue." They are obscene defamations of Jews. Yet, unsuspecting Christians imbibe this poison which corrupts them and perpetuates bigotries against Jews. And they do so in the thick of what they assume to be a religious observance. Compared with this kind of travesty, pornography is only mildly harmful.

Eric Larrabee said that "the true obscenities of American life lie in our vicious public consumption of human suffering in virtually every form and medium. By comparison, the literature of sexual love would seem vastly to be preferred."

As I reflected on Larrabee's phrase "our vicious public consumption of human suffering," and wondered what specifically he might have had in mind, it occurred to me that cruelty is a consumption of suffering, that brutality is a spiritual cannibalism by which we feast on the other person's pain. Sadism produces and consumes the other person's suffering. Thus, every form and medium of communication that promotes a relish for the sufferings of other people rather than a pity for them, that induces joy when some miserable wretch or archenemy is beaten and killed, or that stirs the bloodlust in us is a true obscenity.

But does this occur and are the media in any way responsible for its occurring?

In the July 9, 1967, edition of *The New York Times,* Bosley Crowther stated that there is a growing taste among moviemakers and moviegoers for killing in a gross and bloody manner, for massive and excessive violence—the kind of killing "done by characters whose murderous motivations are morbid, degenerate, and cold. And the eerie thing is that moviegoers are gleefully lapping it up." He referred to such "slaughter-house" films as Robert Aldrich's *The Dirty Dozen* and Sergio Leone's *For a Few Dollars More* as examples of the movies in which mass murder is indulged in gleefully, sadistically, and irrationally to the obvious pleasure of the hordes of people who see them. The showing of these films—and hundreds of similar if less bloody ones that our children will be seeing on television—has, in Crowther's opinion, no redeeming social value.

Some people will say that Crowther is wrong, that violence in movies, books, and television programs releases pent-up hostilities that would otherwise produce antisocial acts. Undoubtedly this is in some cases and to some extent true. The violence we witness in a drama or about which we read becomes a substitute for the violence we might otherwise commit. But there comes that point at which the brutality we witness no longer purges us of cruelty but begins to arouse in us a deeply buried animality that in its latent state was a threat neither to us nor to anyone else. In each of us there are demons so horrible that they are presently inconceivable to us. Everything that we see in anyone else resides in germ in us.

"I am a man," said Terence. "Nothing human is foreign to me." But in most normal people the abnormalities are chained and are weighted down by more powerful interests, emotions, and disciplines. Constant exposure to scenes of excessive and massive cruelty will eventually release cruelty in us.

The Germans under Hitler were essentially no different from any of us, but bit by bit latent cruelty of demonic proportions was released in them by their gradually increasing exposure to brutality. Even if this were not true the films that appeal to our bloodlust would be bad enough. But it is probably true that repeated exposure to sadism uncovers and frees the sadistic impulses that abide in all men. Here, then, on television and in the movies, is a massive and pervasive obscenity—"vicious public consumption of human suffering"—about which we say little and do nothing.

The most monstrous obscenity of our time is the glorification of war and the glamourizing of the military tradition. I am not concerned at the moment about any specific war and am certainly not entering at this time the highly controversial question of United States presence and behavior in Vietnam. Nor am I condemning the young men and women who serve loyally and courageously in our armed forces. Many of them, still doing what they conscientiously believe to be their duty, would say in their own way precisely what I now say in mine. That is, war is the most dehumanizing of all human enterprises, not only in its effect upon those who are killed and wounded, but also in its effect upon those who do the killing and the wounding.

Whatever glamour and romance wars may have had in the past, they have none of it now. Modern war—nuclear war, chemical war, biological war—has brought out all of the hellish factors of human conflict and eliminated all of the noble ones. Therefore, all glorifying of war and all romanticizing of the military tradition is obscene, abhorrent to morality and to virtue. However brutalizing it has become, war remains among us as a method of settling international disputes; and it may be, as some people think, one of the tragic necessities of our time. But it has taken on a new character in our time. Any war in any part of the earth has in it the germs of universal and total destruction.

In modern war one man can by a single, cold, impersonal action destroy a multitude of people or, worse, leave their bodies seared by inextinguishable flame. Every television program, every movie, every bit of literature that exalts modern war and dulls our awareness of its horrors is the most deadly kind of obscenity. Sexual obscenity, even the worst kind of pornography, is a mere nuisance compared with the glamourizing of war.

A Christian people should be concerned wherever anything stunts man's moral, spiritual, and communal development. But they are naïve or hypocritical if they act as though sexual obscenity were the only evil threatening man's becoming man. There are far more subtle and destructive forces playing upon us in this time. And among those forces are the religious and racial bigotry that defames character and denies the other person the right to be what he is, the brutality that feeds itself on human suffering, and the ingenious degeneracy of modern war. This does not mean that we can ignore the destructive effects of sexual degeneracy on society and persons. It does mean that our preoccupation with sex makes us exceedingly vulnerable to obscenities far more dangerous to mankind than his basest sexual offenses.

6
The People's Ether

Amid all the charges and countercharges about the effects of the fast media of communication on the people's character and culture, one fact stands unchallenged: radio and television are lusty, growing giants—immense in their scope, powerful in their claim on the people's time and confidence, and tremendously profitable to their owners and masters. We cannot measure the impact of these media on morality unless we sense their size and their penetration of our culture; for their sheer bulk, as much as anything else, determines their power over our minds, emotions, and behavior. The meaning of these media cannot be understood apart from some comprehension of their mass.

Those people who witnessed the birth of television predicted that the new medium would be the death of radio. They could not have been more mistaken. The growth of the radio industry and the increase in the number of listeners have in some respects been more phenomenal than similar developments in the television industry. In 1965, thirty-one million radio sets were sold in the United States, bringing the total number of sets in operation in the country to nearly 250 million, more than one each for every person in the United States. It is safely estimated that 95 percent of American families have radio sets and that 75 million people use their sets every day. This growth has been more than matched by a simultaneous rise in radio revenue.

The Radio Advertising Bureau reports that radio income for spot advertising in 1965 was more than 250 million dollars. General Motors, Chrysler, and Ford—to mention the advertising of only three major firms—spent a total of 35 million dollars on spot radio advertising in 1964 and 41 million dollars in 1965. We can assume that these well-managed, dollar-concerned companies would not invest such huge sums in radio advertising unless they knew that radio has a vast and growing audience. Local radio stations have mushroomed fivefold in the last decade and the typical local station grosses 150,000 dollars a year and nets 25 to 30,000 dollars. It is reported that Westinghouse paid 10 million dollars for the New York City radio station WINS. Businessmen do not invest that kind of money in a dying enterprise.

There are several reasons why radio confounded the experts and grew rather than lying down supinely and dying before television's challenge. Television itself is one of those reasons. Television increased the people's demand for entertainment and information delivered to them where they are. Television deepened the desire of many people to have a world beyond them breaking in on them at all times, interrupting their solitude and heightening their sense of personal vitality. Where circumstances make the viewing of television impossible or inconvenient—while you are driving a car, fishing a trout stream or figuring an income tax report—radio is the next best way to keep tuned to a seemingly exciting and important world beyond yourself. Thus, unintentionally, television became radio's ally.

Radio's survival and growth were also due to changes that took place within the sets themselves and within the industry. First, radio achieved a mobility that television will probably never be able to match. I remember distinctly the first radio to which I listened when I was twelve or thirteen years old—a battery-powered earphone set that cluttered up a sizable part of our neighbor's living room. It looked like a giant black octopus with elongated tentacles flowing in all directions. The batteries preempted one side of the room and the listeners—straining to hear the voice of Pittsburgh's KDKA—were tied to the immobile set in a way that at first seemed frightening. But radio is quite different today. You can strap a set to your wrist; carry one in your pocket; or, if you wish, have a receiver built into the frames of your eyeglasses. The compactness and power of transistor radios make it possible for you to have a set on your person at all times, and in all this immense country you are never beyond the range of some broadcaster. (Incidentally, four out of five of the transistor sets sold in the United States are made in Japan and the fifth set depends on Japanese-made parts.)

Moreover, the radio industry has capitalized on the fact that we are a mobile society, spending more and more of our time in automobiles. When we include short trips as well as long we can safely estimate that 90 percent of the passenger transportation in this country occurs by automobile and the remainder by bus, train, and plane.

The radio and advertising industries were quick to recognize the commercial significance of one radio salesman's comment that "only radio can hit the consumer on the move." Certainly this is true as far as the driver is concerned. His companions can read or can even watch television broadcasts in the rear of the automobile, but if the driver wants entertainment or information from beyond his car he is restricted to radio. Consequently, it has been estimated, forty-four million adults in the United States listen to car radios every day. Since, as we shall note again, the more affluent and better educated part of our society drifts away from television viewing, it is possible that automobile radios are a more apt symbol of suburbia than television sets. And, in addition to their use in automobiles, radios are being delivered today in a great variety of sizes and shapes to meet numerous human conveniences and thus become indispensable.

Inadvertently television also increased the popularity of radio by compelling it to adopt local flavor and deal with local interests. When television doomed popular coast-to-coast radio programs, the radio industry made its adjustment by adapting its programing to the local scene. In the great metropolitan areas, in fact, this concentration went even further as broadcasters fashioned their programs to the interest of specific groups and developed what has been called "format radio." By this concentration a station gains a recognizable and undeviating character that guarantees to its fans the listening diet they prefer. By serving the local interests that television cannot satisfy, radio stations hold their share of the radio-TV audience.

But if radio has its seventy-five million listeners in the United States on an average day, television will on that same day have one hundred million viewers. If radio sets are present in 95 percent of American homes, so also are television sets. In a thirteen-year period, 1950 to 1963, TV saturation of the country grew from five million to fifty million homes. And one out of four of these homes has two or more television sets. In each of these homes the average viewer spends two hours and forty-one minutes before his TV set each day. Whether he gives broadcasts his undivided attention or not this listening and viewing pattern is an unparalleled phenomenon in human history. If radio received 250 million dollars for spot advertising in 1965, television expects to have a three-billion-dollar advertising program in 1969. To sound and image the television industry has now added color. There were sixteen million color television sets in operation in the United States by the end of 1967, and it is probable that more color sets are now being sold than monochrome sets.

As an entertainment medium, television has passed all other media of communication in the number of people served, and it has also achieved an enormous newscasting effectiveness. A report by Roper Research Associates in April, 1967—"Emerging Profiles of Television and Other Mass Media: Public Attitudes 1959-1967"—stated that 64 percent of the people interviewed for this report preferred television as a source of news over newspapers (55 percent) and radio (28 percent). The significance of television as an informative power can be judged by the fact that it has almost completely killed the newspaper "extra."

In addition to its increasing saturation of the United States, television is now achieving global scope. In an address to the Detroit Economic Club, February 6, 1967, Walter D. Scott, chairman of the board of the National Broadcasting Company, noted that "in 1966 the number of television sets throughout the world rose past the 200 million mark. . . .The truth is that global television has already arrived." News correspondents at their posts in New York, London, and Tokyo can discuss world developments with one another in a live program.

The global aspect of television will increase as we place in space additional and more effective synchronous communication satellites. These satellites, traveling at the same rate as the earth's rotation and therefore always at the same location over the planet, provide the bases by which television broadcasts hop from one continent to another, tying the world into a tight communication knot. Also, films produced in one country are now available in other countries.

According to Scott, N.B.C. International sells "Bonanza" by tape or film to more than seventy countries and it is viewed by an estimated 350 million people every week—more people than any single communication ever produced. There must be some significance in the fact that one-tenth of the world's population views "Bonanza" every week. But when we seek an interpretation of the effect of global television we must not naïvely accept the conclusions suggested by romanticizing sentiment.

We shall need to examine with some care the television mystique now developing in our country, for there is a direct connection between this and authentic morality. At the moment let us merely note that television—which Bishop Hanns Lilje defines as "voice illustrated and made more forceful by image"—has an almost hypnotic and addictive effect on many people. When color is added, the medium's appeal to these people becomes nearly irresistible. The lower the intellectual and educational level, the greater the people's susceptibility to television's lure—an instructive fact to which people concerned about morality in the full sense of the word should pay close attention.

The Roper Research Associates report put the following question to the people it surveyed: "Suppose that you could continue to have only *one* of the following—radio, television, newspapers, or magazines—which one of the four would you *most* want to keep?" The report stated that 53 percent chose television; 26 percent, newspapers; 14 percent, radio; 4 percent, magazines; and 3 percent were undecided. The college educated people interviewed gave the following replies: 39 percent chose television; 38 per cent, newspapers; 13 percent, radio; 8 percent, magazines; and 2 percent made no choice. Thus, the higher the educational level, the lower the appeal of television; but even among the well-educated, according to this poll, television is preferred by 1 percent over all its competitors.

Television and radio, then, are the giants of mass communication. They permeate and saturate our society as do no other media of communication. They are big and getting bigger; rich and getting richer. They receive more of the general public's time and attention in a day than all of the churches receive from their members in a week. Their appeal to the great mass of Americans is immense and some of the ablest minds and biggest budgets in the country are dedicated to making that appeal irresistible. These media contribute directly and indirectly to the moral crisis of our time. Potentially they are both a peril and a promise.

Christian people who are genuinely concerned about authentic morality must help determine whether these media will be a threat to morality or an opportunity. If they move bravely, confidently, and wisely in this field, proving that they are interested in something more than their own churches, something deeper than superficial moralism, Christians will find at their side numerous non-Christian and nonchurch Americans who share with them the desire that mass media contribute in creative ways to man's becoming fully man.

The critics of radio broadcasting have many minor complaints but four principal ones.

First, they insist that as radio becomes bigger and richer its programing becomes poorer. I can bear personal testimony to support this conclusion. Years ago I was a somewhat avid radio fan, but I was weaned by other interests and increasing responsibilities. When I resumed listening to radio with some regularity in preparation for these lectures I was appalled by the amount of trivia, vacuity, and wholly irrational raucousness offered the public by many radio stations in the Chicago area. I realize that these programs are not beamed at my generation or at members of my profession. Perhaps, too, nostalgia has distorted my memory of the quality of the radio programs I once enjoyed. But it seems to me—my 16-year-old son's disclaimers notwithstanding—that radio programing has descended into the depths of noise, meaninglessness, and strident commercialism. Desmond Smith, who is a much closer student of radio than I am, agrees.

The quality of many radio programs can be judged from the

following quotation from Smith's article "American Radio Today—the Listener Be Damned," in the September, 1964, issue of *Harper's:*

> The Situations Wanted column in *Broadcasting*, a leading trade paper, is full of ads like this one: "Way-out jock needs work, record hop genius, real screamer and attention getter, experienced. Write the MOJO-man." Or, "Las Vegas, Nevada's wildman is on the prowl. Catch him while he's hot and be No. 1." On many stations, when a commercial comes along (after every news flash or after every record), the audio engineer is simply instructed to "jack up the audio." One station manager told me, "The teen-agers control the sets, and to a large degree they influence the household spending. If they want a jukebox, that's what we'll give them."

And that, of course, is what the teen-agers, and anyone else who tries to listen to these stations, get—a steady stream of bombastic shrieks and blaring rackets masquerading as music. The programs seem perfectly designed for a generation that, according to comedian Mort Sahl, "is having a nervous breakdown."

Second, the critics say that radio broadcasting is little more than a stream of commercials interrupted by news flashes and recordings. It would be difficult to refute this criticism. Desmond Smith says that commercials have increased from two per hour in the early days of radio to twenty-five an hour in 1963. The format used by many radio stations runs like this: a recording, a commercial, some chatter, a commercial, a news spot, a commercial, and so on. I would guess that this broadcasting format has been devised not to please the listeners but to permit the maximum number of spot advertisements.

There is a place for commercial radio in our regulated free enterprise system, but there is no place for commercial radio that abuses the public interest, the public ownership of the airways, by loading each hour of broadcasting with advertisements that serve the interests of the broadcaster and the advertiser but not necessarily those of the public. The principle on which commercial radio and television rest, and on which broadcasting stations are licensed, is that the listener and viewer pay for information and entertainment by allowing the advertiser to interrupt the program with his sales pitch. This principle collapses when the interests of the salesmen take priority over those of the public. There is a difference between interesting the public in a product and serving the interests of the public. An increasing number of broadcasters seem to be contemptuous of this fact and of the principle on which their right to broadcast rests.

The critics say, third, that the erosion of radio and television broadcasting occurs because so many powerful and influential politicians—congressmen especially—have made heavy financial investments in radio and TV broadcasting firms. Here again I am indebted to Desmond Smith for two illustrations that give this criticism firmness. In his *Harper's* article, Smith quoted James Lawrence Fly, a former chairman of the Federal Communications Commission, describing his appearance before a House committee. "I want to tell you," Fly said, "that the amount of political heat was indescribable. Every station affiliated with a network or that owned a local newspaper would get in touch with its congressmen and senators."

To what extent are congressmen directly involved in radio and television enterprises? Smith stated: "Edmund C. Bunker, president of the Radio Advertising Bureau, and a former lobbyist for one of the broadcasting networks, has estimated that one-third of the members of Congress own radio or television interests." To say that these congressmen cannot vote with complete impartiality on laws affecting the radio and television industry is not to accuse them of being crooks. It is to recognize that they are men. All people in government who can directly or indirectly influence the regulation of broadcasting should be compelled by law to relinquish all financial interests in local and national radio and television before taking office. Such a law should apply to all government officials, from top to bottom. Such a law becomes increasingly imperative as radio and television assert their power over American thought and behavior.

Fourth, the critics say that radio broadcasting is being increasingly victimized by political, social, and religious extremists of the far right, by men who might justly be called patriots for profit and prophets for pay. In the April 15, 1967, issue of *TV Guide,* Neil Hickey wrote about "the strident voices of the so-called Radical

Right which are now heard on more than 10,000 television and radio broadcasts each week in 50 states. . . . Whole sections of the nation are awash with a brand of vitriol which is neither rational political dissent nor the constructive goading of responsible reformers."

Hickey's article, "They Call Themselves Patriots," said that the best known of these extremist groups in radio and TV (primarily in radio) are: Christian Crusade operated by Billy James Hargis of Tulsa, Oklahoma, with 250 radio stations; the Dan Smoot Report with 80 TV and 350 radio stations; Carl McIntire's Twentieth-Century Reformation Hour with 635 radio stations; the Manion Forum with 12 TV and 200 radio stations.

These extremist broadcasters, and hundreds of others of less reputation, are purveyors of fear, hatred, bigotry, and character assassination. Their tools are subtle slander, the whole lie, the half truth, innuendo, distortion. Hickey uses such quotations as the following from these members of the far right:

"Fear is essential to the salvation of the American republic"—Clarence Manion; "The Roman Catholic Church becomes a 'spy system' through the priests"—Carl McIntire; "If we must fall to Communism, I would rather it be over the remains of 10,000,000 charred bodies of which I would be proud to be one"—Manion, again.

Taken as a whole, these members of the Radical Right constitute a multimillion-dollar business, much of their money being raised by radio appeals. They use radio broadcasts to condemn Jews, Catholics, the National Council and World Council of Churches, the Supreme Court, the federal government, the Negro's struggle for racial justice, and to defame the character of individuals. Since these extremists buy time on local stations throughout the country, it is a practical impossibility for any individual to know whether his character has been attacked on the air in a manner contrary to the standards of common ethics and to F.C.C. regulations. And, it is exceedingly difficult—sometimes impossible—for an organization or an individual to secure justice when the extremists defame their character and reputation on local broadcasts.

In November, 1966, the Senate Communications Subcommittee

queried seven hundred TV and radio stations, asking whether they sought responses to controversial statements on their broadcasts; whether invitations to use the station were issued to responsible spokesmen of opposing views; whether the stations had broadcast replies to controversial statements and to attacks on individuals; and, whether, when an individual has been the subject of attack on a broadcast, the station has automatically provided the individual with a transcript or summary of the attack.

As far as I know, the results of this survey have not been made public. But it is a known fact that many radio stations take none of these steps in defense of organizations and individuals that have been subjected to defamation and public ridicule on broadcasts from these stations. Certainly all organizations and individuals have the right to know that they have been the object of attack on radio and television programs. Certainly, also, it is the duty of the stations to inform them of this fact and to provide free time and prime time for their reply.

Whether they agree with the charges against the organizations and individuals or not, the stations' role as public agencies, licensed by government, includes a duty to the whole people. But the facts press us toward the conclusion that the stations are more interested in the revenue they receive from renting time to extremists than they are in justice. When that happens in an agency licensed by the government to use the airways that belong to the people, it becomes the duty of the government to tighten its regulations of broadcasting so that justice may be done.

Any general word we say about the quality of radio broadcasting must allow for exceptions and variations. Some stations are better than other stations. There is still a distinguishable contrast between FM and AM broadcasts in those areas of the country where frequency modulation is available. But this gap is gradually being closed by economic pressures that threaten the quality of FM programing. Many AM stations provide a good coverage of sports and helpful newscasts. But what more can we say about the formats of most radio stations in this country? They are dominated by four groups, none of which is qualified to determine how this powerful instrument can best be used in the public interest. These groups, as we have seen, are: teen-agers, advertisers, politicians having economic interests in broadcasting, and political and religious extremists. By contrast, the influence of universities and colleges, educational and medical institutions, social and civic organizations, the churches, and councils of churches is minimal. The ether—the medium through which the broadcasting medium operates—belongs to the people; but intelligent people, who should be concerned about the quality and effect of radio broadcasting, have surrendered their influence and their power over this medium.

Two of the maladies that afflict radio—triviality and overcommercialism—are shared by television; and, the younger medium has some problems that never troubled the older one. "The boob tube," "the idiot box," "audible wallpaper," "a vast wasteland"—these are some of the many derogatory phrases that have been hurled with considerable justification at television because of the triviality of its programing.

In the March 24, 1965, issue of *The Christian Century,* Desmond Smith wrote: "True, there are some worthwhile shows—in a 20-hour broadcasting day there *ought* to be—yet by and large the prime evening time is dominated by violence, salaciousness, murder, and mayhem." Smith probably had in mind such shows as those produced by the Xerox Corporation, Hallmark Cards, some of the documentaries, newscasts, and sports coverage when he said there are some good shows. But the infrequent good production merely dramatizes how woefully television has failed its promise to the public, how "pitifully unexploited" are its potentials.

The industry is now pushing color to increase its hold on the average viewer and probably also in the hope of winning back that affluent and educated American whose set remains cold all evening. But when image and color are added to sound in the projection of trivia, the trivia are not redeemed but in fact become even more insidious. Color makes the picture more attractive but does not correct the banality of its content.

Television producers say that they are giving the public what the public wants. When the public has no option this claim is difficult to challenge. Insipid themes, shallow plots, raucous musicals, repetitious and maudlin advertisements, blood-soaked melodramas may be what the people want; but we shall not know for sure until some other form of television broadcasting parallels commercial television and gives the people a choice.

If these soporifics *are* what the public wants then television has revealed a vast, deep emptiness in American life; for Americans are consuming day after day huge doses of escapist broadcasting. In either event the pressure is on the church and on all other institutions interested in man's becoming fully man. They should press hard on the one hand for optional television and on the other hand they should soberly reexamine their contribution to the vacuity of American life. If TV is the index of American culture, what must we say about the churches?

The primary deficiency of TV programing is its lack of diversity, not only in subject matter, but especially in quality. I would agree with Lee Loevinger that there is a place for general, low-level commercial TV. In a column titled "Closing the TV Quality Gap" in the April 8, 1967, issue of the *Saturday Review,* Richard L. Tobin quotes Loevinger, a member of the Federal Communications Commission, as saying: "The common man has every right to be common. A demand that popular entertainment conform to the taste standards of critical intellectuals is mere snobbishness. Television is a golden goose that lays scrambled eggs; and it is futile and probably fatal to beat it for not laying caviar. Anyway, more people like scrambled eggs than caviar." But there is a wide gamut of tastes between scrambled eggs and caviar, and the TV menu seldom offers anything other than scrambled eggs. There are two chief reasons why television viewers get so much scrambled eggs.

First, commercial television broadcasting is costly and must therefore be financed by the advertising of products that have a mass appeal: tobacco, automobiles, patent medicines, cosmetics, beer, detergents, food. If the advertisers of these products are to achieve the widest possible coverage they must present programs that have a low-level mass appeal. This means that their programs are designed for mass audiences and not for specialized and educated tastes.

Second, the mass taste is gauged by several research and rating companies which determine from a small but carefully selected sampling of public opinion which programs are most popular. The A. C. Nielsen Company (the Nielsen rating) is widely considered the most reliable of these yardsticks of success or failure. Actually, what these ratings determine is not the TV tastes of the majority of viewers but the tastes of a plurality of viewers. For example, a TV program can collapse, despite the fact that it has ten million loyal viewers, if another program in the same time slot has eleven million viewers. Far from being democratic, the rating system can in fact thwart the interests of the majority of the people. When it is remembered that an infinitesimal sampling is used to determine how many millions of people watch a particular program, the whole rating system becomes suspect.

Let us suppose that the ratings are accurate. Must we then conclude that they are the healthful way of deciding the viewing diet of the American people? Newton N. Minow, former chairman of the Federal Communications Commission, issued some time ago a scathing criticism of the philosophy underlying the rating system. Minow said: "If parents, teachers, and ministers conducted their responsibilities by following the ratings, children would have a steady diet of ice cream, school holidays, and no Sunday School."

Minow is wrong in assuming that TV viewers are children and that someone must make their choices for them. But that is precisely what is now happening. A plurality determines the kind of programs that will be seen by the majority and the plurality is estimated on the basis of a thin sampling. The rating agencies are the gods of American television. They are the makers and breakers of television stars, the authorities before which advertisers bow, the arbiters of American viewing. The custodians of the nation's moral fiber—the churches and all educational and civic institutions—must not ignore the challenge posed by the control which raters and advertisers exercise over the quality of American television.

I suspect that it is futile to urge commercial television to regulate itself as long as it remains commercial and has no competition. The National Association of Broadcasters—called "the single most powerful organization of broadcasters in the country"—has a membership of more than three thousand radio stations and more than four hundred television stations, plus four national radio networks and three TV networks. It is composed, no doubt, of many honorable men serving institutions of unquestionable business integrity.

The N.A.B. has a Radio Code and a Television Code and Seal of Good Practice. Without such self-regulations by the industry itself, radio and television broadcasting would be much worse than it is. But it would be asking too much of human nature to expect the men and organizations most deeply involved in a highly lucrative enterprise to revolutionize that enterprise in the interest of the public. In a pamphlet issued by the N.A.B. this year, Senator John O. Pastore of Rhode Island was quoted as follows: "They [radio and television] are a very, very sensitive media, of course, and have to be guarded in the public interest. . . . The government itself should not censor. We should not intervene or interfere. This responsibility belongs to the leaders in the industry themselves. They should police it."

This is a most surprising word from a senator with as much social consciousness as Pastore often exhibits. To say that the government should not censor is one thing; but to say that it should not intervene or interfere with an industry that uses the people's ether is to encourage the government to be grossly irresponsible. To say that the responsibility of guarding the public interest in radio and television belongs to the industry's leaders is either a statement taken out of context or a sentimentally naïve reading of human nature.

The government—in principle at least—intervenes and interferes with local and national radio and television from the moment specific stations and networks are licensed to operate. However inadequate it may be, the F.C.C. is the government's claim to some control over broadcasting.

The question, then, is not whether the government should intervene—it already does that—but how and to what extent. Moreover, we should not forget that there is a radical difference between the government's interference in the internal affairs of a broadcaster and the government's control over the airways that the broadcaster is licensed to use. As Herbert Hoover said, the ether is a public medium, and the government, in this country at least, is the most reliable representative of the public.

In addition to the commercial blindness that impedes the industry's regulation of itself, there develops within the television industry, and within many of its viewers, an adulation of the medium that makes dispassionate judgment of its effectiveness and its quality difficult. This adulation borders on idolatry and could be called the television mystique. Smith wrote in *The Christian Century*: "It has been said that all television is religious—the difference is only in which god is worshiped." For some people the medium itself becomes the god that is worshiped.

John Goodman, president of the National Broadcasting Company, speaking at Baylor University's World Emphasis Week, April 12, 1967, referred to television as though it were a new messiah. He said: "When communication was a primitive art, the family, or the tribe, was the social unit. As television becomes the basic communication of more and more countries, the whole world will become the community of man. It is no accident that the words 'communication' and 'community' come from the same common root. Television multiplies by millions this face-to-face, human interchange."

This is a fantastic claim. There is no more significance in the fact that the words "communication" and "community" have a common root than in the fact that the words "fratricide" and "fraternity" have a shared root. Communication does not transform automatically into community. A declaration of war, a subpoena, a divorce decree, a death sentence—these are all communications, but they certainly do not produce community. Community, indeed, presumes exactly that kind of communication that television does not provide; that is, dialogue, conversation. It requires spiritual factors over which television has little control. Therefore it is absurd to say, as Goodman did, that "on the simplest level, television viewing is itself an act of community participation." But this opinion, shared even by some of the critics of television broadcasting, has become a part of the television mystique.

Moreover, television acquires among most of its viewers an inordinate credibility. The Roper survey put the following question to the people interviewed: "If you got conflicting or different reports of the same news story from radio, television, the magazines, and the newspapers, which of the four versions would you be most inclined to believe—the one on radio or television or magazines or newspapers?" Of the people interviewed 41 percent found television more believable; 24 percent, newspapers; 8 percent, magazines; 7 percent, radio; and 20 percent did not know or did not answer. These respondents evidently did not know that the more entries a medium has to our consciousness, the more opportunities it has to deceive us. Moreover, many viewers have obviously concluded that when they see the image they see the thing itself—certainly an unwarranted conclusion.

If we will remember "plugola" and "payola," the rigged television quiz shows and the widely discussed use of subliminal advertising, we will then be more suspicious of the believableness of television broadcasting, and certainly much more suspicious of the willingness and the ability of the industry to regulate itself. If you believe that your lucrative business has a messianic role, and if the great masses of the people support you in that belief, you will naturally react arrogantly to all criticism.

Before we attempt some solution of the problems we have raised let us look again at the churches' view of the effect of television on morality. As we said earlier, there is no one view, no firm, documented, clinically tested data to which one can point. But there are clues that should be noted.

Information Service, a publication of the National Council of Churches department of research and survey, issued on April 24, 1954, a comprehensive analysis of the effects of television viewing on children. This analysis needs to be updated, but its summary of three different views is still pertinent. The report first offered five arguments against the subjecting of children to television: Television is a spectator activity; it preempts time that could be better used; it interferes with meals, family schedules, home study, family life; introduces children to crime, violence, questionable tastes and values; and serves parents as a substitute for loving and intelligent supervision.

Over against these criticisms the report put the arguments for television's beneficial effect on children: Television is a "window on the world"; it gives minds unprecedented outreach; it does have "good" programs to choose from; television's episodes of crime and violence are outlets *for* rather than stimuli *to* aggression; television makes the home once again the center of American life.

Third, the report took the middle position that television, like fairy tales or comic books, is neither good nor bad but is "one more addition to the vast complex of stimuli the world presents the growing child, and that the child's response is determined by his character, temperament, emotions, and family and group experience far more than by the content or format of the program." In the light of television's continuing immaturity, its failure to fulfil its promise, its unimaginative underdevelopment, I wonder if this middle position might not be stated differently today.

The position of the National Council of Churches was updated when its general board issued a policy statement in 1963. The pronouncement stated in part:

> Since television, radio, and motion pictures exert powerful influences on the opinions, tastes, and values held among the people of the world, the functioning and effect of the mass media are of inescapable concern to all Christians. [There is] much in mass communication to expand man's horizons, deepen his sympathies, and foster his dignity....But the mass communication that deserves this commendation is forced to compete with programing and advertising that seems often designed to sell products without much regard for what is happening to the people who buy or to the culture which in part is thus being formed. These programs sometimes depend for their success on a scale of values, clearly false....The whole public is responsible for the functioning of mass communication, and the individual Christian, as citizen, is impelled to exert what influence he can to have television and radio operate for the public good.

How can the Christian as citizen discharge his responsibility for the quality of radio and television broadcasting? What leverage does he have? Through what agencies can he impress his definition of good broadcasting on radio and television? The answers to the questions fall into three groups. First, local churches and the radio and television commissions of their denominations and ecumenical councils should learn through experimentation and through the hiring of experts how to exploit the still untapped promises of radio and television.

Liston Pope's condemnation of radio and religious broadcasting in *Christianity and Crisis* (Nov. 14, 1955) still holds true: "In short, many allegedly religious productions are either sentimental or emaciated, or both. In the effort to be appealing they become appalling from the standpoint of sincere and well-founded and full-ranging Christian faith." Pope knew, as he said, that "no matter what is done, religious broadcasts cannot compete successfully with Jackie Gleason for the audience, not even if they give away free trips to the Holy Land or old church pews for use as lawn benches." But he also surmised that radio and television offer the churches teaching and evangelizing opportunities that require radically new, bold, and imaginative formats.

There have been some praiseworthy exceptions but, in the main, Protestant broadcasting has tried to transfer the pulpit and the classroom to the amplifier and the screen. This is a field in which I, for one, am totally inadequate; but there are imaginative young men and women in the churches and in ecumenical posts who should be encouraged to concentrate their services in the area of radio and television and who should be given wide latitude and generous budgets for experimentation in mass communication.

Second, the churches should campaign for optional forms of TV broadcasting that would give the viewer a genuine choice of quality and variety. There are two current possibilities, the first of which is Pay-TV. Operating either through a closed-circuit cable system or through a scrambled broadcast to sets equipped to unscramble sound and image, this alternate makes possible the broadcasting of programs that do not have a mass appeal but that are interesting to select groups of people. Pay-TV has moved beyond the experimental stage but has run into governmental roadblocks. In an article in the October, 1964, issue of *The Atlantic*—"Why Suppress Pay-TV? The Fight in California"—Sylvester L. Weaver, Jr., president of Subscription Television, Inc., said that at that time his company had thirty thousand subscribers and expected to have a million by the early 1970's.

But Pay-TV has been vigorously resisted by commercial broadcasters and by their friends in politics. In 1958 the Columbia Broadcasting System, Inc., published and distributed widely a pamphlet titled "Free Television and the American People." This attempt to kill Pay-TV in its infancy stated: "It costs as much as $1,209,900,000 a year to provide throughout every day and far into the night the wide variety of programs from which . . . 42 million families choose by a mere flick of a switch what they want to see and hear—entertainment, news, discussions on matters of social or political controversy, programs of education, religion, and general culture. It all costs the viewer nothing." The cold fact is that every cent of the fantastic cost of commercial television is paid by the American public.

In a book titled *Television and Society* by Harry J. Skornia (McGraw-Hill Book Co., 1965), the author makes the following estimates of the cost of commercial television to the average family: Amortization of the cost of the TV set, $110 to $250; amount of advertising costs to be allocated to each set per year, $75; electrical and repair costs additional. It is a safe guess that commercial television costs the average American family two hundred dollars a year. For many people this is a big bite out of the family budget and is far from "nothing."

However, there is another possibility called Public Television. Some months ago the Carnegie Commission on Educational Television suggested that a network of noncommercial TV stations to be called Public Television be financed by the federal government. The network would incorporate National Educational Television and would produce programs of unusual quality in entertainment, education, and news. President Lyndon B. Johnson picked up this suggestion and proposed to Congress that such a network be established at an initial cost of ten million dollars in governmental investment. The proposal recognizes that there are two kinds of television audiences—mass and select—and that the needs of the select audience are not being served. Although Public Television will surely need strong safeguards against political pressure, this alternate to commercial TV seems a wise one.

The churches should support this proposal. (Indeed, it should also be supported by commercial broadcasters, since it would relieve them of pressure to put cultural and public affairs programs in prime time and might—to the commercial broadcasters' profit—re-cultivate the television habit among the affluent and the better educated people.)

If the churches are genuinely interested in morality in the broad, deep sense of the word, they should adopt, without changing a word, the announced goal of the Carnegie Commission on Educational Television. That goal reads: "If we were to sum up our proposal with all the brevity at our command we would say that what we recommend is freedom. We seek freedom from the constraints, however necessary in their context, of commercial television. We seek for educational television stations freedom from the pressures of inadequate funds. We seek for the artist, the technician, the journalist, the scholar, and the public servant freedom to create, freedom to innovate, freedom to be heard in this most far-reaching medium. We seek for the citizen freedom to view, to see programs that the present system by its incompleteness denies him."

The constant concept in this declaration is freedom; and freedom, we have concluded, is the habitat of authentic morality.

Finally, the churches should help untie the hands of the Federal Communications Commission and stiffen its spine. During the 1959-60 disclosures of quiz show "fixing" and "payola," a weak Federal Communications Commission could have become a stronger one. But it is difficult to draw the line between a healthfully strong F.C.C. and a dangerously strong one. So the F.C.C.'s request for stricter regulation of television was not received favorably. Even so, the commission can exert pressure on a station through its power to review a station's license every three years. The F.C.C., then, does have power, but it appears reluctant to use it.

A commission exercising total control over broadcasting would be a general censor, and that catastrophe, of course, we do not want. But why should we have a commission emasculated by politicians, by advertisers, and by broadcasters? If the F.C.C. is to do its duty somewhere between these extremes it must be encouraged to do so. Here the churches have a role to play and that role, it has now been proved, can be effective.

Nearly three years ago the United Church of Christ office of communication filed with the F.C.C. a petition challenging renewal of licenses for television stations WLBT and WJTV in Jackson, Mississippi, on the ground that the stations failed to provide service and "courtesy" for Negroes, though they make up 40 percent or more of the area's population.

The Commission, as we reported this event in *The Christian Century*, "dismissed the office of communication petition for a public hearing and declined to order such a hearing, holding that the public has no standing before the commission except in cases in which it is economically involved." The United Church appealed to the United States court of appeals, which ruled that the public does have an interest in broadcasting policies and does have standing before the F.C.C., whether or not it is financially involved. The F.C.C. put one of the stations on probation and renewed the license of the other.

The United Church of Christ action proved that the churches have standing before the Federal Communications Commission in a charge against a broadcasting station whether or not they are financially involved. It proved that the policies of a station can be successfully challenged and that a docile F.C.C. can be aroused. It would be a mistake for the churches to continually harass the commission; but when the commission defaults its duty, it should be forcefully reminded of its role as the guardian of the people's ether.

When he was chairman of the F.C.C., Newton Minow said: "Under the law television is a private industry subject to federal regulations because it uses scarce and valuable public channels on the air." The F.C.C., the broadcasters, the advertisers, and the politicians must not be permitted to forget that fact. If they do, the churches will have no one to blame but themselves.

7
Morality and Madison Avenue

Several New York City streets have become symbols by which we identify and refer to major aspects of American life. Everyone knows that Wall Street is not merely a narrow passageway at the tip of Manhattan Island but a vast financial empire; that Fifth Avenue is the acme of elegant and expensive shops; that Park Avenue means luxurious urban residences.

In recent years Madison Avenue, which *Time* magazine calls "a street named Desire," has become a euphemism for mass advertising through numerous and powerful agencies. Actually, only twenty-five of the forty-two major advertising agencies in the United States are located in Manhattan and only seven of these have offices on Madison Avenue. But this concentration was sufficient to make someone call this avenue the capital of mass advertising, and the stereotype stuck. Therefore, to speak about morality and Madison Avenue is to ask what effect advertising has on man's becoming fully man.

Let us first state concretely the obvious fact that advertising is big business. In addition to the forty-two major advertising agencies with budgets running between twenty-five million dollars and nearly four hundred million dollars a year there are more than 450 other agencies, all engaged in a dog-eat-dog business.

There is probably no more competitive business in the nation than advertising. The in-fighting in this institution—the plagiarizing of ideas, the forays one company makes on another in the search for professional talent, the rivalry for clients—often becomes ruthless, and the lack of moral sensitivity within the industry is inevitably passed on to a public over which advertising has great influence. In a business in which the loss of one major client can drive an agency to its knees, in which one failure to anticipate unpredictable shifts in the fickle public mood can mean the loss of millions of dollars, in which rumors about declining prestige can ruin an agency overnight, it can be expected that competitiveness will often exceed ethical bounds. And it can be expected that unethical practices within the industry will determine the character of that industry's approach to the public.

Each year the number of consumers in the United States increases by three million. Each year multiplied millions of Americans switch from one brand to another—not on the basis of quality or cost but largely under the motivation of whims. To capture these new customers and those whose buying habits are in constant flux, United States business and industry spend more than thirteen billion dollars each year in advertising. The figure was twelve billion in 1962, thirteen billion in 1964, and it is steadily rising. It is estimated that the average business must budget one dollar in advertising for every seventy dollars in sales. This means that when you pay three thousand dollars for a new automobile, you pay forty-two dollars for the cost of advertising that automobile.

The average American today is exposed to sixteen hundred advertisements each day and ten thousand television commercials a year. Of course, the average American develops psychological defenses against this pressure. He preserves his sanity and what is left of his pocketbook by learning to turn off and tune out the "Buy! Buy! Buy!" cries that are hurled at him by the printed page, the billboard, radio, and television. But the customer's resistance incites redoubled efforts on the part of advertising agencies.

The volume increase that occurs during radio and television commercials is one of the simpler devices by which the advertiser pursues the listener who for one reason or another leaves the room during a commercial. The pursuit is far more subtle than this. Most of the major advertising agencies have professionally trained sociologists, economists, statisticians, and psychologists on their staff, constantly studying how to crash or slip through the public's guard against advertising.

There is nothing new about this principle of sociologically and psychologically directed advertising. For more than a generation advertisers have been exploring the human mind and spirit to discover more effective ways to get the message of their product across. Vance Packard's well-known exposé of the advertising world, *The Hidden Persuaders* (1957), dealt with the new phenomenon in advertising that emerged following World War II:

> . . . large-scale efforts being made, often with impressive success, to channel our unthinking habits, our purchasing decisions, and our thought processes by the use of insights gleaned from psychiatry and the social sciences. Typically these efforts take place beneath our level of awareness; so that the appeals which move us are often, in a sense, "hidden." The result is that many of us are being influenced, and manipulated, far more than we realize, in the patterns of our everyday lives.[1]

The appeal of advertising, Packard said, is not to "the conscious, rational level of our minds," but to "the level of prejudices, assumptions, fears, emotional promptings, and so on" and to an even deeper level, "where we not only are not aware of our true attitudes and feelings but would not discuss them if we could."

Long before the sociological and psychological approach to advertising became a science, and in itself a big business, wise salesmen knew—as they said—that it is the sizzle and not the cow that sells the steak. They knew that even in dealing with intelligent people they had to appeal to something deeper than the rational mind. In fact, in most sales to intellectuals the rational mind must be by-passed by flattery. For example, I bought my set of the *Encyclopaedia Britannica* because I wanted it and because the salesman "carelessly" let drop the confession that selling a person with my prestige would help him with other sales in the community. So when Ernest Dichter, Ph.D., director of the Institution for Motivational Research, says, "To women, don't sell shoes—sell lovely feet!" or when the Pepsi-Cola Company shows us pictures of gay young people and invites us to join "the Pepsi generation" or the automobile industry's advertisements employ sexual allusions,

---

[1]Used by permission of David McKay Company, Inc.

the appeal is to insights clever salesmen have always employed. The difference now is that a vast, powerful, well-financed industry has systematized, intensified, and universalized this ancient principle of salesmanship.

To what extent the advertising industry has succumbed to an even more pernicious form of advertising I do not know. But I do know that it is tempted to manipulate the viewer's lower levels of apprehension electronically and that it now has the ability to do so. I am referring, of course, to what has been called the "subliminal, subcontrollable, subconscious" approach to advertising and to what could be called electronic hypnosis.

In 1957 the Subliminal Projection Company of New York City announced that it could condition spectators by showing "unseen" advertising messages on movie and television screens in 1/3000th-of-a-second flashes interspersed in a conventional film. In a six weeks experiment conducted by the company in a New Jersey theater the human beings who unwittingly served as guinea pigs purchased 18 percent more Coca-Cola and 57 percent more popcorn than usual. Think of the diabolical uses to which this technique can be put not only by advertisers but also by despotic rulers of a country. Subliminal conditioning has such dangerous possibilities that even the Subliminal Projection Company suggested that it should be put under federal government control.

When the possibility of electronic brainwashing was first announced and it was evident that this could be the means toward the ultimate robotization of man, *The Christian Century* replied editorially as follows: "Massive retaliation seems to be in order. We have drawn up a list, in case the monster is universalized: Don't go to movies. Turn off TV. Buy no brands that do not display a 'No Subliminal Projection Advertising' affidavit. Refuse to discuss ways for the churches to redeem this thing for their own use ('Decide for Christ Tonite!' 'Go to Church Sunday!'). Plan a down payment on some sort of Walden Pond."

Unfortunately, Walden Ponds are scarce, in fact, nonexistent, today. If man is to remain free and is to fulfil himself in a complex and crowded world he must outlaw those devices that capture his subconscious being without his awareness of what is happening to it. Advertisers should be rigidly prohibited from using any form of electronic hypnosis, any device that captures the subconscious man and uses him for its purposes without his consent. The invasion of privacy is one of the most serious problems of our society, but there is a more pernicious threat—the electronic invasion of man's subconscious being.

We see, then, that advertising is big business, that it envelops the people, penetrates their minds, exploits their emotions as no other business does. Madison Avenue uses the vast resources of the other streets in a highly competitive, systematized, aggressive campaign "that makes music at the cash registers by stimulating the public desire to acquire goods." It is the medium that pours life into all the other media upon which all businesses are to some extent dependent. It would be a mistake to underestimate the impact of Madison Avenue on Main Street, to ignore what advertising does to our freedom, our tastes, our moods, our conduct, and our morality. It is obvious that a force so powerful and so pervasive plays a major role in fashioning that society and that culture in which we are trying to produce an authentic morality. Is this force beneficial or destructive?

The British historian Arnold Toynbee is reported to have said, "I cannot think of any circumstance in which advertising would not be evil."

I do not know under what circumstances Toynbee made that extravagant statement. The context in which it was made may have modified it to something closer to rational criticism. But I do know that I cannot agree with it. I can think of a number of circumstances in which advertising is not only not evil but is positively good. Take this afternoon's *Chicago Daily News,* for example. In case after case businesses tell prospective customers that they have specific goods for sale, describe the quality of the goods, and plainly designate the price.

As I leaf through the *Chicago Daily News* for July 27, 1967, I note of course the kind of ads that made Toynbee shriek. Here is one by Walgreen Drug Stores: "Come to Walgreen's to enter the 'just wonderful' sweepstakes! Win Al Hirt and have a blast!" This ad pushes the gambling, something-for-nothing, gimmick currently used by many chain stores and gasoline distributors to attract customers. This gimmick is in no way related to the merchandise these businesses sell or to the quality of that merchandise. But the annoying gimmick—annoying to many customers and a nuisance to most proprietors—does have an effect on the price of the merchandise and on the amount of taxes paid to the federal government. And those of us who do not want to participate in lotteries or who are otherwise annoyed by trading stamps and sweepstakes devices are trapped into helping pay for those who do. Or, here is an ad that implies one can drink a pint of I. W. Harper whiskey and at the same time enjoy the pleasures of fishing and golfing. A third ad—full page—suggests a direct connection between masculinity, wide-open spaces, good health, and the smoking of Marlboro cigarettes.

But there are other advertisements. Here is a two-page Kroger ad for sundry groceries, with the various items and their prices plainly specified; a Carson Pirie Scott & Company announcement giving full details on mini refrigerators and freezers; a "Pre-back-to-school" Montgomery Ward sale on "young men's suits designed for campus or career"; a Marshall Field & Company presentation of shirts and trousers for juvenile boys; a Pan Am advertisement of tours from Chicago to various European cities.

Such ads are beneficial not only because they keep the wheels of industry and finance turning but even more because they announce to the public, without pressure, what is available, at what quality, and at what price. This is an important social function, the primary purpose of advertising—not to propagandize but to inform. To the extent that advertising falls within this pattern, to that extent it escapes Toynbee's indictment. It is beneficial, not evil.

Nor can I forget that the enterprise in which I am engaged as the editor of *The Christian Century* receives a part of its income from advertising, primarily the advertising of books. Indeed, we consider that kind of advertising a part of our moral responsibility and our service to our subscribers. If we allowed advertising to make up the bulk of our magazine or if we accepted the advertisements we now reject because they appear to us distasteful and untrustworthy, then we would refute our own editorial policy and make something evil out of something good. In the January 4, 1967, issue of *The Christian Century* we severely criticized *Life* magazine's advertising policy. A Lutheran minister had drawn our attention to the fact that the December 16, 1966, issue of *Life* had no editorial comment on the Christmas theme but had 32½ pages of advertising of alcoholic beverages. We said:

> Secular magazines as well as religious ones have a moral responsibility for the people's sobriety. We do not expect such magazines to preach total abstinence or to refuse all advertisements for alcoholic beverages. We do expect them to exercise good judgment, moderation, and a sense of public duty. When a magazine going into millions of homes devotes nearly one-third of its space in a single issue to liquor ads it defaults its public charge in a crass pursuit of the almighty dollar.

Advertising is not inherently evil. It is instrumental and it can therefore be put to good uses or bad, depending on the character and motivation of those who use it.

There are good reasons for suspecting that advertising originating at the local level has more integrity than mass advertising produced by agencies for national distribution. The generalization is dangerous but when allowance is made for exceptions it has merit. The local merchant who produces his own ads, or who hires local talent to do so, is subject to an immediate test of his accountability. Moreover, mass advertising must resort to vague abstractions that are nothing more than commercial fiction as it vainly attempts to prove the merit of one detergent or cigarette or analgesic over another.

By and large, mass advertising does not attempt to describe the product; rather, by the use of romantic rhetoric and fanciful pictures, it tries to affix an irresistible aura of distinctiveness to the product. Since the local merchant usually sells all brands, his advertisements must be specific, and descriptions of his merchandise must be more concrete than those of mass advertising. Generally, mass advertising omits all specific reference to price, but the local merchant must tell prospective customers what prices he expects for his goods. For these reasons locally produced advertising appears more reliable than professionally produced mass advertising. But whether this thesis has merit or not, my concern from this point on will be with mass advertising, for it is at this level that advertising helps form the society and culture in which man must struggle to become fully man.

In his book *The Hidden Persuaders,* Vance Packard identified himself as a member of the Loring Chase Congregational Church in New Canaan, Connecticut. I presume that his reason for doing so was to say obliquely that his questions about the morality of mass advertising had rootage in the Christian ethic. Whether that is so or not, his questions are those that Christians should raise about this universal, pervasive, and subtle molder of our culture and of our personal tastes and habits. I therefore repeat some of his questions from his chapter on "The Question of Morality":

> What are the implications of all this persuasion in terms of our existing morality? What does it mean for the national morality to have so many powerfully influential people taking a manipulative attitude toward our society? Some of these persuaders, in their energetic endeavors to sway our actions, seem to fall unwittingly into the attitude that man exists to be manipulated. . . .
>
> What is the morality of the practice of encouraging housewives to be nonrational and impulsive in buying the family food? What is the morality of playing upon hidden weaknesses and frailties—such as our anxieties, aggressive feelings, dread of nonconformity, and infantile hangovers—to sell products? . . . . What is the morality of manipulating small children even before they reach the age where they are legally responsible for their actions? What is the morality of treating voters like customers, and child customers seeking father images at that? What is the morality of exploiting our deepest sexual sensitivities and yearnings for commercial purposes? What is the morality of appealing for our charity by playing upon our secret desires for self-enhancement? What is the morality of developing in the public an attitude of wastefulness toward national resources by encouraging the "psychological obsolescence" of products already in use?[2]

The raising of these questions is itself an indictment of the advertising industry. Is that indictment just?

Let us take up first the criticism of mass advertising for its lack of good taste. Since taste is subjective, since it has no fixed stand-

---

[2] *Op. cit.*

ards, this is a difficult criticism to substantiate. What annoys one reader, listener, or viewer does not offend another. Some people are offended by the elaborate and graphic television, radio, and slick magazine advertisements of deodorants, laxatives, toilet tissues, sanitary napkins, and other intimate items of our personal lives. This does not mean that these people necessarily think such things bad or the human need for them shameful. Rather, in their opinion, there are areas of privacy and modesty that should not be rudely invaded by boorish advertisements.

This criticism of advertising is more general than might be thought in this anything-goes age. In the Roper survey, 69 percent of the people questioned said that many television commercials are done in poor taste; 59 percent said that they are usually too noisy and loud; 54 percent said that these commercials advertise things that should not be advertised. Criticisms of mass advertising on the basis of good taste are usually brushed aside as prudishness. But prudery, like good taste, is subjective. It has no fixed standards. To the boorish, all good taste is prudery.

The advertising industry also defends itself against the charge of bad taste with the rejoinder that advertising is much more discreet than it was fifty years ago. The industry points to the fact that in our grandfathers' day all sorts of patent medicines were openly advertised as panaceas and that this practice has now been discontinued in the advertising world. This is true, of course; but the industry can hardly take credit for doing what the federal government through the Food and Drug Administration compelled it to do. Wherever it is left to itself the advertising industry is tempted to do whatever is necessary to get the public's attention, even though it has to offend the public to do it.

A far more serious criticism of mass advertising contends that the industry deceives the public, not only by withholding vital information about products, but also by making misleading and even false claims. The Roper survey stated that 73 percent of the people it interviewed believe that "advertisers making false claims is a serious problem." A few illustrations will be sufficient.

In an article called "The Vitamin Healers" in the December 16, 1965, issue of *The Reporter,* Ralph Lee Smith cited a Food and

Drug Administration report that so-called health foods cost ten million Americans over five hundred million dollars a year. Said Smith: "Urging the public on is a satellite industry which specializes in the dissemination of dubious, misleading, and false health information. And responding to the insatiable popular interest in these matters, a number of publishers and radio and television stations have become involved."

Carey McWilliams, editor of *The Nation,* tells how overweight Americans were persuaded to pay sixteen million dollars for four million boxes of Regimen tablets—officially described as "largely worthless"—between 1956 and 1963 (*The Christian Century,* June 22, 1966). The television campaign for Regimen involved the use of testimonials by professional actors and actresses who were paid approximately one thousand dollars for each pound lost over a period of three or four weeks. One actress testified that she had been paid eleven thousand dollars for losing fifteen pounds. She admitted that she had to live on cucumbers, celery, black coffee, and barbiturates for the last part of the test. Viewers were led to believe the weight loss was due to Regimen; whereas, it was in fact due to starvation diets.

This past summer Donald F. Turner, assistant attorney general in charge of the antitrust division of the Justice Department, was quoted by William J. Easton of the *Chicago Daily News* as saying of advertising: "I don't think present methods give consumers the information they need to make a rational choice. . . . As it is now, people can sell an inferior bargain through the use of heavy advertising."

Mass advertising has the power to deceive the public without openly misrepresenting the quality of products. In its approach to many Americans the advertising industry can rely on the television mystique and the authority of printed words and pictures to convey claims that are not explicitly stated. As *Time* magazine put it: "In the fast-turning world of packaged goods where advertising budgets often run higher than the cost of production and a blindfolded customer can scarcely distinguish between competing brands, it is the adman's task to find and exploit any slight difference, real or imagined, in his client's product."

Admen have risen to the challenge. They have developed to a fine art their ability to make their client's product appear infinitely superior to a rival product, even though there is no material difference between the two. The story of the competition between the four main producers of analgesics illustrates the deceptive extravagance used in competing advertisements.

Morton Mintz of the Washington *Post* reported in the summer of 1967 that the Federal Trade Commission and the Food and Drug Administration are now seeking to eliminate deceptive advertisement claims for nonprescriptive pain-killing drugs. The producers of these drugs engage in a ninety-million-dollar-a-year advertisting campaign as each seeks to capture the major part of a five hundred-million-dollar-a-year retail business. The Federal Trade Commission proposes to regulate the advertising of Anacin, Bufferin, Excedrin, St. Joseph Aspirin, and Bayer Aspirin by prohibiting claims for efficacy or safety not approved by the Food and Drug Administration, by forbidding false comparisons with rival products, and by banning claims that specific ingredients have beneficial effects, unless the ingredients are identified by their common names. A ninety-million-dollar advertising business rides on fictitious claims that one or the other pain-killing drug is superior to the rest when in fact there is little substantial difference in them. This advertising campaign not only deceives the public but also adds 18 percent to the cost of the drugs.

Third, mass advertising simultaneously encourages wastefulness and cultivates a materialistic philosophy of life. The industry's creed and gospel, its moral imperative, is consumption. You would think as you listen to some commercials that you are anti-American, that you are subverting the nation's economy, if you drive last year's model, wear last year's shoes, or refuse to use the new soap.

The goal of the advertiser is to create within the consumer a nagging discontentment and to plant in his mind a powerful suggestion that the advertised product will satisfy that discontentment. The advertising industry's anthropology—whether definitely formulated and expressed or not—holds that man is a bundle of unsatisfied and unsuspected wants that can be appeased only by material things.

Clair M. Cook—formerly editor of *Walking Together*, an organ of the Religion and Labor Council of America—once wrote: "Other institutions among the few which are truly 'instruments of social control' have tried to improve us and to develop qualities of social value, as with the church, the schools, the law, the free enterprise system. But advertising has no social motivation, no social goals, and no social responsibility." Cook quoted Charles M. Potter, Yale historian, who in his *People of Plenty* said: "This lack of institutional responsibility is a basic cause for concern about the role of advertising [especially since it has] joined the charmed circle of institutions which fix the values and standards of society."

Cook and Potter may have taken in too much territory with their blanket statements, but they put their fingers on one of the most crucial problems of those institutions that want man to be fully man.

More and more, mass advertising assumes a principal role in shaping the mores of the American people. Yet this institution has little social concern and few principles that commend themselves to Christian approval. It has at its disposal more money than the whole nation puts into its elementary and high school public education, far more than all the contributions to all the nation's churches and synagogues. Preachers, Sunday School teachers, and religious literature receive only a pitiful fraction of the time and attention commanded by the powerful advertising enterprise. Most little children know commercial jingles and slogans long before they learn Sunday School songs and Bible verses. They have a much closer identity with commercial symbols than with biblical characters. Increasingly, mass advertising becomes the innovator of our fashions, the creator of our tastes and manners, the subverter of our morals.

It requires only a moment's reflection to convince us that the philosophy by which this industry operates is antithetical to almost everything we have been taught as Christians. It appeals to and accentuates the sensual and materialistic nature of man.

The values exalted by mass advertising are youth, sexual attractiveness, romance, social prestige, affluence, and power. These are the ultimate "good things," the gods, of mass advertising. Its three commandments are: "Thou shalt covet; thou shalt buy; thou shalt consume." To entice man's obedience to these commandments, mass advertising frequently profanes man's spirituality, his sexuality, his love of his family, his personal ambition, his patriotism. Little is too sordid, nothing is too sacred to be used by the advertising industry if it will make the American people buy and consume.

If the mass advertising industry took seriously for one day one sentence from Jesus Christ, the industry would collapse. For that sentence contradicts the whole philosophy of mass advertising: "Take heed, and beware of all covetousness; for a man's life does not consist in the abundance of his possessions."

Let me suggest, however, that there is an aspect of this problem that we must not hypocritically ignore. It is only fair to ask to what extent mass advertising makes us what we are and to what extent it merely reveals what we are. In *The British Weekly* for June 8, 1967, a column called "Peter Parson's Log" commented on truth in advertising campaigns and said: "Alas! there is already more truth in advertising than many of us like to admit. To scan the advertisements is to see how accurately the hidden persuaders have gauged our values, standards, and desires—and our own estimate of ourselves." There is an unpleasant amount of truth in this suggestion that mass advertising corrupts us by uncovering our corruption.

George Norman Douglas once said, "You can tell the ideals of a nation by its advertisements." If this is true, where have our religious and educational institutions been during the past generation? Why have they failed their roles as the molders of American morality? As I have shown, mass advertising is a powerful and effective producer of fashions, tastes, manners, and morals. But it is more than that. It is a mirror reflecting what we are: And what we see there is not consoling to those of us who desire for the people the mature and meaningful manhood that we have seen in Jesus Christ.

8
This Barbaric Invasion

Nearly forty years ago René Clair, a French film director, wrote: "It is too late for those who love the art of moving pictures to deplore the effects of this barbaric invasion. All they can do is try to cut their losses." By the phrase, "this barbaric invasion," he was referring to the advent of talking motion pictures—the addition of sound to moving images—and to the threat this development posed to the devotees of silent films. To these people the silent film was an ultimate art form and the advent of sound film was a boorish, unthinkable, and temporary intrusion. But René Clair took a more realistic and practical view of the situation. "The talking film," he said, "exists, and those skeptics who prophesy a short reign for it will die themselves long before it's over." Therefore, to cut the losses, he dedicated his career to seeing what could be done with the new combination of sound and image.

The French director's phrase can be applied to the whole motion picture industry. All of it—moving image, sound, color, wide screen, third dimension—is a barbaric invasion of twentieth-century thought, manners, conduct, religion, morality. Indeed, I can think of no other mechanical device that has had as profound and pervasive an influence on our culture as have the motion picture camera and projector. But the critics—including the churches—have met this invasion with much deploring and with little attempt "to cut their losses." They forgot that the barbarian always enters the stagnant situation as a potentially constructive as well as destructive force.

The Ostrogoths and the Visigoths did great harm when they overran Rome, but they also contributed a new vitality to the people of a moribund civilization. The cinematic industry was that kind of barbaric invasion. It released in the country an enormous vitality that had both creative and destructive possibilities. Ivor Montagu, who has had a distinguished career in almost every area of motion pictures and television, understood both the peril and the promise of motion pictures. As he summed up the two generations of motion picture history, he wrote:

> From one point of view, a tale of mortality. As they say in the North Country, from rags to riches and back to rags. The peep show replaced by the goggle-box, after pausing at the picture palace on the way. But from another point of view it is quite a different story. The cinema was, and is, a new invention, an extension of man's powers. It has given him new means of studying, and assimilating to his knowledge, reality—new means of moving, influencing, communicating with his fellowmen.

Unfortunately, the church—particularly in the early years of the movies—saw the threat but not the promise. Motion pictures were viewed as a clear and present danger to church attendance, to the hold of the church on the minds of the people, and to the attitudes and behavior that the church had cultivated among the people.

In the first and second decades of this century motion pictures brought to still predominantly rural and small town America the outside world of which journalism, traveling vaudeville shows, and Chautauqua had only given hints. For many churchmen in these areas it was a strange and frightening world that broke upon their communities through the Celluloid invader, and the invader therefore had to be resisted. I grew up in such a town at such a time. Since I was not in these early days of my youth under the guardianship of the church, O'Dowd's Theater and the Opera House were favorite haunts to which I gained access through the pennies I earned selling newspapers and metal scrap. Nevertheless I felt, even in my detachment from the church, the frown it had for the immoral motion picture business.

In fairness it must be stated that from the beginning the motion picture industry seemed bent on a deliberate policy of antagonizing the churches. Quite early in this century the Hollywood colony began to flout the mores and moralities of the nation not only in its cinematic productions but even more in the private lives of the colony. By the end of World War I, Hollywood had achieved a reputation as the capital of Bacchanalia, the center of unbridled revelry, prostitution, adultery, divorce, drinking, dope-addiction, the seduction of young women by the promise of glamourous careers. That this was a deserved reputation was proved in the early 1920's by the "Fatty" Arbuckle rape case, the unsolved murder of William Desmond Taylor, the revelation of Wallace Reid's drug-addiction—to mention only three of the more notorious instances.

The churches reacted in a characteristic fashion: They deplored the advent of the barbarian, the bowing down of the nation toward its new Sodom and Gomorrah, the surrender of the nation's standards of morality to a colony of men and women who had in the main no concern for morality. So they deplored but did not cut their losses; they rebuked the cinematic barbarian but made little effort to convert its tremendous energies to their purposes.

They protested the moral quality of the films produced by Hollywood. And, their protests helped produce the motion picture industry's self-regulating body, the Motion Picture Producers and Distributors of America, which was organized in 1922. This body appointed to its presidency Presbyterian elder Will H. Hays, formerly chairman of the Republican National Committee and United States postmaster general in the Harding administration. M.P.P.D.A. soon became known as "the Hays Office." Having confidently entrusted the censoring of Hollywood films to a man of such sterling reputation and respectability, the churches relaxed; and the motion picture industry soon slipped back into its old ways. The churches were also deceived into believing that they were winning the day for Christian morality when the industry periodically produced biblically based extravaganzas, but that is a matter we must examine in more detail later.

The barbaric invasion is a reality; it will not go away. The radical changes occurring in the industry today are evidences not of the industry's mortality but of its metamorphosis.

When television began to move into the lead in the early 1950's as the nation's number one entertainer, a deep pessimism descended on Hollywood. Weekly attendance at the movie houses across the country dropped to one-half of what it had been at its peak. The importation of foreign films also cut deep into the Hollywood monopoly in movie production.

But television's increasing demand for material produced a market for the numerous old movies, stored in the industry's film libraries, and eventually for the industry's newer productions. The significance of this new relation between the television and motion picture industries was dramatized in September, 1966, when sixty million people watched the American Broadcasting Company's presentation of *The Bridge on the River Kwai*. For this rental of this film and for a second use at a later date the American Broadcasting Company reportedly paid Columbia Pictures two million dollars. Shortly afterwards two of the networks announced arrangements for renting 113 films from three studios for ninety-two million dollars.

Increasingly Hollywood will produce motion pictures for original release on television. The motion picture industry has struck a seemingly inexhaustible bonanza.

If the church had cause in the past to be concerned about the culture-shaping power of motion pictures, it has cause in the present to be doubly concerned. The people will be seeing more motion pictures in the future, not less. What is the continuing effect of this barbaric invasion on the people's morality? Is there any way in which the cinema can be made to fulfil its promise as "an extension of man's powers" rather than its threat to man's maturity and to his fulness as a moral creature? Are these still pertinent questions or have the churches conceded that their view of moral man has been challenged by a foe for which they are no match?

Several years ago I had an opportunity to converse briefly with an executive of one of the major motion picture studios who happened to be visiting Charleston, West Virginia. During the course of our conversation, I told the executive that I had stopped going to the movies because I found most films tasteless, immature, and boring. His reply surprised me. He asked: "How old are you?" When I told him that I was forty-three years old, he said: "We are not interested in your opinion of movies or in the opinion of anyone else over forty years old. We fashion our movies for young people, not for old; for the coming generation, not for the departing one." I could have guessed it, but it was helpful to have this authoritative confirmation of the fact that motion pictures, by and large, are devised to capture the youth of the country. As I write this, for example, my sixteen-year-old son is at a local theater, watching *Grand Prix,* a film that will no doubt thrill him but would be for me prolonged and painful boredom.

From a strictly commercial viewpoint, the movie producers are obviously appealing to the right side of the generation gap. And this concentration on youth is certainly not in itself pernicious or reprehensible. Such judgments become relevant only as we examine the lures by which the motion picture industry attracts youth and the values it offers them in exchange for their money, time, and adulation.

The fare that Hollywood offers the under-forty generation is varied, but it bulks large in two categories—sex and violence. We assume that this is so, but does the assumption rest on hard evidence? I turned to the motion picture advertisements in the *Chicago Sun-Times* for August 4, 1967, and found the assumption abundantly confirmed. I ran my eye over the following titles, all appealing to sexual interests: *Hollywood World of Flesh, Once Upon a Knight, Strange Bedfellows, A Guide for Married Men, Woman Times 7, The Touch of Her Flesh, Highway Pickup.* And the appeal to the human interest in violence was represented by such films as *El Dorado, For a Few Dollars More, You Only Live Twice, The Dirty Dozen, Hell's Angels on Wheels.* These pages of the *Sun-Times* offered options of a different quality and character: *A Man for All Seasons, The Taming of the Shrew, The Sound of Music, Dr. Zhivago.* These were the notable exceptions; the heavy accent in theater after theater was on sex and violence—not romance and adventure but raw sex and crass violence, sex without love and violence without redemptive purpose.

The industry has concluded that sexuality, violence, crime, and horror pay at the box office and that virtue, chastity, sacrifice, and peace do not pay at the box office. It has concluded that this is what the public wants and therefore what the public should get.

If this were solely my opinion, I would be suspicious of it, for I have a professional bias that needs to be corrected by people whose vocational commitments are different from my own. But I find that more and more of the motion picture critics are disgusted by the narrow and neurotic focus of most motion pictures. For example, movie critic Hollis Alpert wrote in the *Saturday Review* for August 5, 1967:

> The conviction that crime pays off at the box office is firmly entrenched in Hollywood, and it is a melancholy fact that far more of our nation's hoodlums, gangsters, and wild ones in general have been enshrined cinematically than our more worthy historical figures. Few indeed are the films built around philanthropists, pacifists, and scientific wonder-workers, but from Billy the Kid to Dillinger, a long line of antiheroes has stalked the screen, guns in hands. It might be an interesting project for some student of cinema economics to tot up the hundreds of millions spent by studioes to illustrate historic crime, and perhaps balance this with the sickly sums spent on portraying artists, statesmen, notable teachers, and other benefactors of society, with which our history is also filled. No doubt about it—Hollywood is firmly crime-oriented, because it knows that the public will buy violence; it always has and presumably it always will.

I am not suggesting that sex and violence should not be treated in motion pictures. They should be portrayed, for they are major parts of the fabric of life. If we exclude from the screen all novels, dramas, histories, and biographies in which sex and violence are major themes, then, of course, we deprive the screen of the best fiction, the best history, and the best biography. In fact, ban sex and violence from the screen and you ban the Bible.

The charge to be brought against Hollywood is not that it handles such themes. It cannot mirror life without doing so. No, the charges against Hollywood are two: It gives to sex and violence an inordinate attention and thereby implies that this is all that life is. And, second, intentionally or not, it glorifies raw sex and violence as preferred ways of life.

Man is more than a sexual and violent creature. He has other powers and other needs. Some of the Hollywood productions prove that the movie industry is not ignorant of this fact.

During the time I was writing these words, I watched *The Spiral*

Road on television. It was certainly not a great motion picture, but I watched it because it featured Rock Hudson, about whom I had heard but had not seen, and Burl Ives, whom I knew through recordings of his folk songs. In this film the hero's discovery of his need for God and for other people was too pat, too moralistic, too homiletical for my taste. Nevertheless the themes of genuine love and service, of folly and pride, of arrogance and human interdependence, of sex and violence were mixed in proper proportions. It was a good motion picture, even though it lacked greatness in the artistic handling of its thematic material. It was good because it was realistic and the realism was whole. Sex and violence—intensified in this instance by restraint—belonged in this film but they took their proper place in the context of equally real and equally indispensable themes.

Man has a natural, intense, and in itself not unwholesome interest in his animal and sensual nature. That interest becomes morbid to the extent that it is extracted from and obliterates all other interests. By definition, a monster is "an animal or plant departing greatly in form or structure from the usual type of the species." Psychologically, man becomes a monster when any part of his intellectual or emotional nature becomes so excessive that all other parts are dwarfed. Human preoccupation with sex and with violence, a preoccupation that detaches these natural interests from their proper contexts, is a monstrosity; and all forms of communication that cultivate and appeal to this preoccupation with animality and sexuality are participants in a monster-producing business. On this ground the motion picture industry must in general be condemned.

There are notable exceptions, but taken as a whole the industry extracts and inflates animal and sensual man. It does so by the volume of its material devoted to this part of man's life and by the glorification of man's lower nature. We have no right to ask the industry to eliminate depictions of sex and violence, but since we are interested in the whole man it is our duty to remind Hollywood as forcefully as we can that life is more than the bed and the gun.

How can the barbaric invasion be tamed and be made to serve the best and the most promising nature of man? Let us consider several present attempts to answer this question, all of them thus far inadequate. First, a brief word about films produced by and for the churches through such church-related organizations as Concordia Films, Family Films, and Cathedral Films. Although some of the films produced by the churches for church consumption no doubt serve a good purpose, most of them are maudlin, moralistic, sermonic, and artistically poor.

I agree with movie critic Arthur Knight, who wrote (*Saturday Review*, November 19, 1966): "Church films . . . have rarely had the stamina to make it on their own in the movie houses. Too often they have been weakly produced, concentrating on messages designed for a specific flock rather than raising their sights to matters of broad, general interest."

Knight mentioned two films that all of us would want to include as exceptions to his general criticism: *Martin Luther*, now nearly fifteen years old, and *A Time for Burning*. Perhaps we might also add *Question 7* and *Parable*, but it would be difficult to think of other church-produced films with sufficient quality and excitement to rival what flows from Hollywood week after week. The churches cannot command the artistic competence and financial resources required for genuine competition with commercial films. This is a way of saying that the churches cannot eliminate or modify the impact of commercial films on public morality by producing superior films that have both religious content and popular appeal.

Perhaps my pessimistic view of the efficacy of church-produced films is due to a personal bias against all attempts to transfer the Christian gospel directly and specifically from words to film. I confess that I have an aversion to films with a message, and this aversion is compounded when the transfer is bluntly and slovenly executed, as so often happens in church films.

This aversion is strongest when I am compelled to witness attempts to portray Jesus of Nazareth cinematically. In my opinion it has not been done and cannot be done successfully either by church or commercial producers. I understand that orthodox Muslims consider it a sacrilege to make pictorial representations of the prophet Muhammad. Pictorial representations of Jesus of Nazareth are certainly no sacrilege unless they are used to defame him. But such representations are so often a travesty that a moratorium on such portrayals would be welcome. Who can believe these pale, blond, blue-eyed, ethereal Christs that float through biblical films, speaking holy words in unctuous tones? But this view, as I have confessed, is a personal bias that does not have general support.

The Hollywood-produced biblical films can be dismissed with similar brevity. There is ground for the suspicion that in the early years of motion picture history Hollywood produced biblical features to divert the churches' criticism of the colony's moral conduct and its permissive code. But it was discovered (perhaps Cecil B. DeMille was the discoverer) that biblical extravaganzas could be the carriers for sex, violence, and glamour. DeMille's pseudobiblical spectacles included *The Ten Commandments, King of Kings, The Sign of the Cross, Samson and Delilah,* and others.

DeMille made full use of the discovery that elaborate orgies could be hinted at in the movie houses of the nation without protest from the churches if the orgies were presented as authentic and pertinent religious history. So the lucrative combination gave the people glimpses of Sodom and Gomorrah and the pious satisfaction of having witnessed a biblical drama. But these biblically based spectacles were gigantic frauds: they actually gave the people little sex and far less religion.

However, we must apply more crucial tests than this one to Hollywood's religious films and to those that now come to us from other film capitals. There remains in many Americans—despite their secularity—a pious or a superstitious streak that prevents their applying to religious films the same tough tests that they would apply to cinematic translations of novels, dramas, histories, and biographies. This is a mistake. When cherished literature is turned into film, we have the right to ask whether the translation is faithful, artistic, authentic, effective, and entertaining. For Christians—and also for Jews, as far as the Old Testament is concerned—this right becomes a duty whenever the Bible provides scenarios for motion pictures. Since for us the Bible is sacred rather than ordinary literature, it is especially important that the screen's versions of the Bible be authentic and faithful translations.

Most pseudobiblical films fail one or both of these tests. Let us note three of the best known illustrations of this fact. The first illustration is DeMille's second version of *The Ten Commandments,* which I saw about ten years ago under great family pressure. Technically, this film was an amazing spectacle; but artistically, and as a cinematic translation of the Bible, it was a colossally mechanical and literalistic farce that made a mockery of the God who is spirit. *The Greatest Story Ever Told*—the George Stevens production about which so much was written—was endorsed by many churchmen but to the sharper critics this three-and-a-half hour, twenty-million-dollar, star-studded film was a spectacular combination of cinematic incompetence and biblical travesty.

In his review for *The Christian Century* (April 21, 1965), Fred Myers said that *The Greatest Story Ever Told* was "inane script, put together from a mishmash of hybrid translations of the Bible, and a potpourri of random half-thoughts about the gospel story." Myers pointed out such incongruities as these: The woman taken in adultery was both Mary Magdalene and the Mary who anointed Jesus; Jews recited psalms from the Revised Standard Version of the Bible; words from the apostle Paul were put in the mouth of Jesus.

A more recent biblical spectacle—*The Bible . . . in the Beginning*—received a favorable word from a film critic who knows cinematic art but an unfavorable word from a critic who understands the meaning of the Scriptures. Arthur Knight of the *Saturday Review* staff said of *The Bible . . . in the Beginning:* It is "as fine a version of the Old Testament as we shall ever see in movies, combining the child's freshness of vision with the deep-rooted understanding of two mature men to provide a satisfying and disturbing quasi-religious experience." But *The Christian Century* reviewer of this film—Malcolm Boyd—was not so kind, or perhaps we should say that he was more objective than Knight. Boyd found in John Huston's *The Bible . . . in the Beginning* "all the earmarks of a DeMille spectacular . . . over-literalistic, pseudo-historical portrayals of poetry and myth."

Christians have an interest in artistic competence, in technical and dramatic effectiveness, in wholesome entertainment. But when the motion picture industry presents the Bible in film the primary and crucial concern of Christians should be the faithfulness and authenticity of the translation of the Scriptures. Unfortunately clergymen have been cajoled and bamboozled into endorsing pseudobiblical films that distort the biblical account and, far more dangerous, corrupt the biblical message.

One other religious film of our time demands our attention, not because it fits the pattern I have described but because it appears to be an exception and, I might add, a rebuke to my cynical view of religious films. I am referring to Pier Paolo Pasolini's *The Gospel According to St. Matthew. The Christian Century,* which shares some of my aversion to biblical films, gave this film two predominantly favorable reviews.

The first was by Associate Editor Martin E. Marty, who saw the Italian version of the film in Rome while he was attending the closing session of Vatican Council II. A snatch from Dr. Marty's review (Dec. 13, 1964) is sufficient evidence of the extent to which he was captured by this "first gospel on film." Marty wrote: "Everything then turns on Jesus, well played by Enrique Irazoqui, a black-eyed 'Jesus' who shares with Pasolini the responsibility for removing so many images of the pale, frail Jesus we have come to know from DeMille or from Sunday School 'bathrobe' movies. He heals, he smiles (rarely, and usually only for children), he leads, he consoles, more often he scolds, he dies, he rises."

The second review was by J. Robert Nelson, professor of theology at Boston University School of Theology and a *Century* editor at large. Dr. Nelson wrote (March 16, 1966): "All right, you theologically sophisticated cynics, you aesthetic skeptics, you cinemaphiles and cinemaphobes alike. Line up with me before the confessional. We have some contrition to express to Italian film director Pier Paolo Pasolini, and then some thanksgiving. For years we have greeted every biblical movie with appropriate sneers. With justifiable disdain we have derided the phony piety and sensate spectacle of all the glorified Sunday School pageants. We have debunked DeMille and stoned even Stevens. And, especially with respect to the life of Jesus, we have said it couldn't be done on film. But it has been done!"

I will withhold final judgment until I see for myself. But if, as these two reliable critics say, Pasolini has combined cinematic artistry and fidelity to the gospel, then we are faced with a most perplexing question: Why was this accomplishment produced by an avowed Communist and "public sinner" who was inspired by Pope John XXIII, when Hollywood, advised in religious matters by some of the nation's leading churchmen, has so repeatedly failed?

If church-produced movies actually contribute little to authentic morality and if pseudobiblical commercial films are in this respect a liability, what help can we expect from the barbaric invasion? What kind of films can help man become fully man? To this question I can give three affirmative answers.

First, modern man, driven by the hectic pace of life in a complex society, threatened by enormous problems that endanger his life, his society and his sanity, needs the relaxation that can be provided by skilfully executed films that are dedicated solely to entertainment. A motion picture does not need to have a message in order to be therapeutic. Indeed, there is in our day a great need for films that deliberately avoid the controversial issues, the seemingly insoluble problems, and that let us escape into the land of humor, fantasy, and romance. Such films as *The Sound of Music, Mary Poppins, The Russians Are Coming; the Russians Are Coming,* and *The Pink Panther* wash away the cares that might otherwise crush us. They are not exits through which we make morbid escapes from life's realities, but on the contrary are refreshing reminders that life has other dimensions than drudgery, fatigue, and terror.

Second, the so-called "problem films"—movies that are not documentaries but that deal with social, psychological, and international issues—can serve the cause of authentic morality, provided of course that such films rest on reliable research and are competently executed.

When the Motion Picture Production Code was revised in 1956, Tom F. Driver said (*The Christian Century,* January 2, 1957) that the changes in the ban on "drug-addiction and illicit drug traffic, prostitution, abortion, and the kidnapping of children . . . are for the most part salutary, since they reflect a growing awareness of certain problems which cannot benefit from public silence."

Since that time movies have dealt with incest, sexual impotence, nymphomania, voyeurism, necrophilia, schizophrenia, venereal disease, dope-addiction, religious bigotry, racial prejudice. Obviously the lifting of the ban on such subjects could be demonic rather than salutary. If prostitution is glamourized, if emotional sickness is ridiculed, if sexual aberrations are endorsed, if bigotry and prejudice are justified and encouraged, then by lifting the ban on these themes we open a box of demons. But it is no less true that the nobler aspects of human life can also be treated perfidiously. The quality of a "problem film" is not determined by the subject with which it deals but by the relevance of that subject to man's total being, by the competence with which the theme is handled cinematically, and by the purposes motivating the producer.

The motion picture industry deserves credit for producing a number of significant films under this heading. Such films as the following come quickly to mind: *Gentlemen's Agreement, On the Beach, All the King's Men, The Ugly American, Fail Safe, The Man with the Golden Arm,* and an increasingly long list of films that touch the racial problem in the United States with various degrees of boldness and realism—among them *Pinky, Intruder in the Dust, The Defiant Ones, Raisin in the Sun,* and *Nothing But a Man.* (Surprisingly, however, the industry has not yet built a masterwork around the theme that has for so long dominated American thought.) These "problem films" are immensely beneficial in enlarging our perspective, deepening our understanding, and challenging our consciences. But it would be a mistake for religious, civic, and educational institutions to rely on the motion picture industry to conduct the crusade that belongs to them.

Ultimately the industry will make its decision about programing on a financial basis and on no other. In a day when feature films of all kinds are becoming progressively costly and "problem films" have lost the attractiveness of shock and surprise, it may become increasingly difficult to finance "problem films." If a producer has ten million dollars to invest in a picture, it is much safer to put it in a James Bond-type thriller than in a serious treatment of a grave social controversy. Abby Mann, author of *Judgment at Nuremberg,* believes that resources for such films are already drying up. He said: "We are at a crisis point in subject matter. The literature of the cinema should reflect the times we live in, yet no one is willing to finance serious, tough-minded films on, say, the race crisis."

If Mann is correct, the supply of socially sensitive films with a broad popular appeal is at best uncertain. "Problem films" are no substitute for an awakened social conscience in the church.

When Laurence Olivier's *Henry V,* one of the truly great motion pictures of the past generation, was shown in Boston some years ago, the word "bawdy house" was cut from the film during Sunday showings but allowed during the weekdays. This ludicrous censorship symbolizes all that has been bad about the church's reaction to the motion picture industry: inconsistent; ostentatiously pious and moralistic; absurdly petty in its complaints; winning small battles at the expense of big ones.

Alternately preoccupied with trivia and lulled by Hollywood's pseudobiblical spectaculars, focusing its energies on morals rather than morality, the church addressed to the motion picture industry a superficial criticism and a bland challenge. Concentrating their criticism on profanity, nudity, and offenses against the prestige of the church, religious forces offered little resistance to the violence and the materialistic values that saturated much of the Hollywood production. A jingle repeated by Driver about a decade ago illustrated the warped view of the church:

> This film is under official ban
> Because the hero utters "damn."
> Well, we will go to see another,
> And watch a gangster shoot his mother.

Today, late in the game, some churchmen are beginning to ask the right questions and make the right demands of the motion picture industry. This trend is evident in the awards granted in recent years to commercial films by the National Council of Churches Broadcasting and Film Commission and by the National Catholic Office for Motion Pictures, successor to the Legion of Decency. Although I disagree with specific selections made by these two groups, I agree with the underlying principles that motivated their choices during the three years they have made awards. In its first venture in this field the Broadcasting and Film Commission honored three 1964 films: *Becket,* in the category treating "religious subject matter, whether biblical, historical, or contemporary, with accuracy, pertinence and moral value"; *Fate Is the Hunter* for "portraying American life and culture in the light of Christian ideals"; and *Fail Safe* for "reflecting the predicament and hope of man." These may not have been the best selections for 1964, but they indicated the emergence of new criteria for the appraisal of commercial films by church groups.

The 1965 Protestant awards went to the following films for excellence in various categories: *The Pawnbroker, Nothing But a Man, The Eleanor Roosevelt Story, Patch of Blue,* and *Sound of Music.* The National Catholic Office for Motion Pictures honored *Darling* as the "best film for mature audiences"; *Sound of Music* as the "best film for general audiences"; *Juliet of the Spirits* as the "best foreign language film"; and *World Without Sun* as the "best film of educational value."

These selections and the startling refusal of both groups to honor *The Greatest Story Ever Told* were dramatic proof that some churchmen are applying new measurements and standards to commercial films. Whether Hollywood got the message or not, these awards were clear evidence that some men in the church were no longer supinely surrendering to the film colony's view of religion or of religious artistry and that these men would not stop with the usual, predictable criticisms and the lame challenges but would demand from the industry new kinds of faithfulness and excellence.

The demand for "artistic merit within the Christian perspective" that was evident in the 1965 awards was even stronger in the 1966 selections by the Broadcasting and Film Commission. *The Bible . . . in the Beginning* was ignored and awards were given to *A Man for All Seasons, The Sand Pebbles, Who's Afraid of Virginia Woolf?, The Russians Are Coming, the Russians Are Coming,* and to two films especially appropriate for children: *And Now, Miguel* and *Born Free.* Since the Broadcasting and Film Commission has no category for foreign films, a special 1966 award was granted to Pasolini's *The Gospel According to St. Matthew.* (*A Man for All Seasons* received a joint Protestant-Roman Catholic award.)

What is indicated by these selections, and by the radically new attitude they reveal in the minds of churchmen? Only a few years ago Christian spokesmen would have condemned *Who's Afraid of Virginia Woolf?* for its profanity and its sexuality. But today a group of responsible churchmen honors this film—to the great astonishment of many Christians—because, as they said, it "reveals the struggle for integrity and wholeness that resists the temptation to live within fantasy and deceit, and to turn instead to courageous acceptance of the responsibility of maturity."

A clue as to what these selections mean, what is happening to official Protestant—and Roman Catholic—attitudes toward commercial motion pictures is best given by comments from two members of the National Council's B.F.C. nominating panel.

After the 1965 awards were announced, James M. Wall, Methodist minister and editor of *Christian Advocate,* wrote: "Surely, in honoring *Pawnbroker,* the B.F.C. is saying to film directors that there is at least one segment of the U. S. church public which is willing to acknowledge the commercial film as a medium for the work of artists. If we in the church are alert to this opportunity, we can point our constituency away from thinking of film simply as escapist entertainment toward an awareness of the potential the film holds as a conveyor of grace." But if this is to occur, as Wall said earlier, Christians must "permit the film to operate as an art form and not be shackled by legalistic moral strictures" (*Christian Advocate,* March 10, 1966).

The second clue came from Episcopal clergyman Malcolm Boyd, now with the Episcopal Society for Cultural and Racial Unity, who predicted the church's trend toward a mature relationship to film long before it began. In an article, "All Films Are Theological" (*The Christian Century,* December 1, 1954), Boyd wrote: "From the first products of Mary Pickford, D. W. Griffith, and Charles Chaplin to the best current output of Huston, Wyler, and Stevens, theology is woven through the film like a thread through a tapestry. It is equally interesting when the artists are aware of this thread and when they are not. God is everlasting God, men are men, art is art, standards are standards, sin is sin. . . . Religion never leaves off in any area of life. The question is not: Is this a religious film? Rather, the question is, or should be: What religious significance can this film have for me?"

I must express a strong personal disagreement with some of Boyd's criticisms and opinions in other areas, but he deserves strong commendation for sensing and for helping produce a new critique of commercial films.

In summary I would say that the motion picture industry has no more obligation to serve the institutional or religious interests of the church than it has to serve the political or ideological interests of the state. Its business is not propaganda of any sort; but its business—like that of other art forms—is to entertain and enlighten man's mind and spirit by a faithful portrayal of the whole man in all his relations within the disciplines imposed by the peculiarities of this form.

The industry does not owe the church pseudoreligious extravaganzas, fawning surrender to sectarian or moralistic codes or even films that are pointedly and meritoriously religious. Its duty is to fulfil its own highest potential as a unique art form, extending and deepening man's knowledge of his whole self in all his dimensions of terror, hope, weakness, and promise. If the screen is a faithful mirror of true man, if it dramatizes his worst and his best and all the strange mixtures of worst and best, it will contribute to authentic morality.

James Wall was wrong when he wrote (*The Christian Century*, June 16, 1965): "We can begin our search for an answer by confessing that we no longer have any general principles to bring to bear on a given film." By "we" he meant Christians, and Christians do have general principles to apply to all things. Indeed, Wall refuted himself by going on to say: "Each film must be examined in the light of what it says about and to the human situation as the Christian community knows that situation to be revealed in Jesus Christ."

In spite of himself, Wall has stated a principle and it is a good one. Put in the form of questions, the principle that Christian people should apply to all films from the motion picture industry is this: Do the films focus on people? Do they in any way and to some degree aid the transformation of people into persons? Do they in some way increase the range of that freedom that is moral man's habitat? Do the films, even when they depict man at his worst, stand the test of that love that we Christians have seen fully revealed in Jesus Christ? Do they, in a word, contribute to man's becoming fully man? The church should forswear carping criticisms of a petty and superficial nature and should challenge the motion picture industry to make its own unique contribution to the emergence of authentic morality.

9
On Legislating Morals

Thus far, we have defined morality in terms that give it a new focus and precision. We have explored the effect of the mass media—particularly those means of communication that are commonly labeled "fast" or "electronic"—on morality. We have dealt at some length with the question of censorship and its relation to the freedom that is morality's habitat. With these concrete illustrations behind us, we can now ask what roles law and religion can play in enabling communication to promote man's becoming truly man. How do we as citizens and as a Christian people help put mass communication at the disposal of authentic morality? To answer these questions we are in this chapter exploring the relation between morality, the media, and the law. In the concluding chapter we shall consider the duties and opportunities of the Christian in controlling and utilizing the mass media. We are asking first, then, about the role of the law in the interplay between mass media and morality.

Since, in this chapter, we are concerned with man's laws rather than with God's, we should note at once that man's laws are both good and bad, beneficial and harmful. Man's laws can encourage and foster the good, happy, creative life or blight and stultify it. This being true, we have said nothing for or against man's private or collective behavior when we have cited what the law allows or what it forbids. If we had assumed that man's laws are justified by their sheer existence or antiquity and therefore unalterable, then for good or ill we would still be bound by all the rigid codes that governed our Puritan ancestors. Surely the most conservative among us would not want to live in a society in which the minutiae of personal life were as closely governed as they were in Puritan times. What would be our condition if we had allowed the writing of no new laws during the past three hundred years?

So, whatever we may think about the absolute and invariable character of God's laws, we have to concede that there is a certain tentativeness about man's laws. They must always be open to reappraisal in the light of man's changing circumstances, always subject to modification and cancellation. We are liable to think that those approved or accepted patterns of human conduct on which we opened our eyes when we first became socially conscious are sacred and sufficient. When that is our mood, our view of the law tends to become caked around the familiar and inherited patterns. But times change and the structures of man's laws must always be sufficiently elastic to allow changing laws to meet changing needs.

Certainly one of the most dramatic and massive changes that has occurred in our society in the past half century has been the change in the form and scope of communications. The coming of the electronic media has necessitated the writing of many new laws and has compelled the sloughing off or the ignoring of some old ones. This process will continue. It requires therefore that we decide as a Christian people where we are to apply such powers as are ours in the casting off of old laws and the adoption of new ones to achieve a beneficial control of mass media, a control that contributes to the abundant life God wills for man. Let us approach this task by seeing first whether we can lay down some general principles to govern the Christian's attitude toward the law and particularly toward the law's effect on the mass media.

Few clichés are more popular with men and more frequently summoned to their aid in argument than two that wholly contradict each other. The first of these clichés says, "You can't legislate morals." The second says, "There ought to be a law!" Although these two popular maxims represent conflicting attitudes toward the law, most men slip from one to the other with the greatest ease, according to the flow of their prejudices and what at the moment they are trying to prove. For example, a racist who is arguing against open-housing legislation will eventually cap his argument with the words, "You can't legislate morals." But if the same man is condemning juvenile delinquency or obscenity in the motion pictures or desecration of the flag he will probably declare with a great deal of passion that there should be tough legal restraints against such antisocial practices. Obviously this is a clear case of fallacious reasoning, a loose and contradictory use of slogans. You cannot have it both ways at the same time.

Nevertheless, though these clichés are usually employed in a slipshod, contradictory manner, there is some validity in each of them. When we understand what they intend to say, we have to concede that each of the sayings has merit. Taken together, they imply, in a word, that there is a time to legislate and a time to refrain from legislating. There are some good ends that can be obtained by the law and some that cannot be obtained by the law. There are aspects of mass communication that a responsible society should regulate by an enforceable code, and there are other aspects that can only be worsened by law. So, let us use these two often misapplied slogans as texts and see where they lead us. It may prove that each of the texts is true in its own way.

People who say that morals cannot be legislated are correct if by the word "morals" they mean—as they sometimes do—man's sentimental and religious thoughts and feelings. If in this context morality means our hopes, aspirations, devotions, and affections, then, of course, these inner parts of man's being cannot be changed by the law or by the law's penalty. We have a superb illustration of this truth in two cases that came before the United States Supreme Court nearly a generation ago.

In the first decision the court held that public schools have the right to demand that the children of Jehovah's Witnesses salute the United States flag. Having been taught that saluting the flag is idolatrous, the children continued to disobey their teachers. Although it was backed by the might of the United States, the high court was impotent before these little children who obeyed the religious teachings passed on to them by their parents. The heart of a little child blunted the will of United States law. Eventually, the case reached the Supreme Court a second time. This time the court wisely reversed itself, confessing that what the country wanted from the children—love and respect for flag and country—it could not coerce.

The law can prevent the burning of the flag, or make the penalty most inconvenient for those who do; but, despite all the authority behind it, the law cannot compel anyone to respect the flag. In the days of the Inquisition many a man was tortured—sometimes to death—for heresy. In some cases the torturing may have brought forth a confession of faith, but we can take a cynical view of confessions of faith that come by such routes. The law reaches an impassable frontier at the border of man's soul.

When this interpretation of this cliché is laid before us in such plain language, we cannot escape the wisdom of it. At other times, though, our concepts of religious and patriotic feelings drift back into the Puritan notion that man's internal condition can and should be coerced by governmental and ecclesiastical edicts. When we are in this mood, we conclude that if an attitude is wrong it can and should be set right by the exercise of some kind of force. But there are human tastes, quirks, opinions that—though to most people deplorable—can never be eliminated by legislation. Indeed, when the law intrudes into this area of man's being, when it tries to alter his opinions and feelings, the probability is that it will violate his person without improving his character. The purpose of the law is not to make man good, not even to make him just, but to protect him from injustice.

At this point a fine distinction needs to be made between the ineffectiveness of legislation as a corrective of man's internal being and the effectiveness of social legislation in safeguarding men against injustice. The law, for example, cannot make Negroes and whites—or whites and whites for that matter—love one another or enjoy mutual company. This is an area of life in which the law is impotent. But the law can establish justice in desegregated housing and schooling. The law cannot compel men to enjoy good drama

rather than bad or make them despise radio and television programs suffused in violence and salaciousness. But the law can determine that the people's ether shall not be preempted by this kind of broadcasting, that there shall be abundant alternatives for viewing and listening, that substantial air time shall be reserved in the people's interest for religious and educational programing, and that young children whose parents are irresponsible shall be protected against programs that assault their tender character. The law is not concerned with men's thoughts and feelings or with men's attitudes toward one another but with that behavior in which the right or special interest of one impinges on the right of another. This means that there are broad areas in which the law must operate in governing the mass media.

In his book *Folkways,* the American economist and sociologist William Graham Sumner devised a maxim that has been a favorite with men who resist the changing of social patterns by legislation. His maxim sounds quite similar to the cliché against legislating morals but in fact drives toward a quite different conclusion. Sumner said that "stateways cannot change folkways," by which he meant that legislation cannot change the general patterns of social conduct. This, of course, is not true. There are numerous historical illustrations of the fact that stateways can change the mores of a people for good or for evil. In Turkey, for example, under the vigorous and aggressive leadership of Kemal Atatürk, the people swung rapidly from a medieval to a modern culture. Under the rule of Adolf Hitler, Germans reverted to a barbaric conduct in their dealings with the Jews. And in the southern part of the United States the 1954 Supreme Court decision against racially segregated schools slowly but surely gains acceptance even among that diminishing part of the people that has experienced no change in racial attitude.

Spinoza said quite correctly that "he who seeks to regulate everything by law is more likely to arouse vices than to reform them." And this is a part of what we are letting the popular cliché teach us as we consider how and to what extent to bring the law to bear on the mass media. The cliché gives us one of the fundamental reasons for our argument in an earlier chapter against the censorship that tries to standardize the character of other men according to our definition of good and bad. Our society has the right and the need to regulate the mass media and to do so by the exercise of law; but it blunders badly when it presumes to restrict—except for most grievous causes—what through the media of communication the people are privileged to see and to hear. If we should discover unquestionable proof in cause-and-effect cases that a certain kind of broadcasting—let us say of violence or of lasciviousness—generally results in imitative action, then we will need to reexamine the necessity for censorship. Until then we should treat quite seriously Spinoza's warning against superfluous laws.

But Spinoza was only partly correct. To what he rightly said we can add that he who seeks to regulate too little by law guarantees anarchy. If one of our clichés—one of our two texts—correctly says, "You can't legislate morals," the other is equally correct in saying, "There ought to be a law!" Granted that most people who say this desire the wrong laws for the wrong reasons, it remains true that both culture and society root themselves in law. For, though the law does not produce character, the character of civilized men tends to express itself by law. Intelligent, civilized men have the good sense not to trust themselves too much. They know that what they aspire to they will generally not do unless they put themselves under mutually accepted bonds.

In his book *Talks on American Law*, Harold J. Bergman gave the following definition: "Law is an expression of man's rational and moral nature, and . . . any particular law must be interpreted in the light of the rational and moral purposes which it is designed to fulfill." This may not be the only helpful way to define the nature of law, but it applies perfectly as we ask about the relation of law to the mass media.

What is our purpose, what do we want to accomplish when we attempt to bring the mass media under stricter legal control? We already have our answer to this question: we seek authentic morality—a morality defined by its focus on people, by its concern with the transforming of people into persons, by its demand that man be allowed the freedom in which the full person can develop. This definition, we have said, conforms to man's highest rational, spiritual, and ethical nature. So we are asking how the mass media can be made to serve this end and the role that law plays in bringing this about.

We have said with sufficient emphasis that one of the primary duties of the law in its relation to mass communication and authentic morality is to provide the mass media the widest freedom consistent with public safety—not because the owners and operators of the media necessarily deserve such freedom but because the people do, and because, bereft of this habitat, they cannot be truly moral.

We should, therefore, take a dim view of censorship; and we should oppose any governmental encroachment on the mass media that would make them the servants of a particular religious or political system or of the government itself. There is room in our democracy for a government-sponsored television network, but there should be no room for governmental domination of television or for a governmental network so powerful that it enters into crippling competition with private television enterprises. When Thomas Jefferson's phrase, "freedom of the press," became a part of the First Amendment to the United States Constitution, it referred narrowly to newspapers, journals, tracts, and books. Today the word "press" covers all of the new media of communication that have evolved since Jefferson's day. So we are saying that the privileges and immunities the Constitution once attributed to the press are now the properties of all forms of instantaneous communication.

However, in this country it was decided a long time ago that the whole purpose in maintaining a free press (the published variety) is to protect and to foster a free people. It is not the press that is sacred but the people it serves. The right to publish and to distribute publications does not derive from those who publish but from a free people's elementary right to be fully informed. The phrase about the freedom of the press—one of only five rights specifically mentioned in the First Amendment—was not included to protect the special interests of such publishers as Benjamin Franklin but to guarantee to the whole people their complete right to all knowledge and opinion.

In a little book I have found most helpful—*Your Rugged Constitution,* written by Bruce and Esther Findlay and published by Stanford University Press—there is an interpretation of freedom of press and speech that I believe should be pushed to a deeper level. The Findlays say: "Congress cannot stop you from saying, writing, or printing almost anything you like." The implication is that the right to free expression is in itself a fundamental right, and undoubtedly this is one of the intended objectives of this amendment. But the people's free and full right to knowledge and opinion is the basic one. It has been said that if one man's opinion differs from that of everyone else in the world, he should have the right to express it. This is true, for his opinion might be correct. But he would not need to express his opinion to enlighten himself. It is the people's need for his possibly true opinion that gives him the warrant to express it. There will not be many occasions in this country when great masses of the people will be concerned about their right to say whatever they want to say. But their need to see, read, and hear whatever they will is a daily one. It is this basic right that the First Amendment protects, and to do so it must guarantee the freedom of the press not only in its old forms but in its new ones.

However, the Constitution of the United States is very wisely based on the assumption that men are not angels and that they therefore cannot be trusted to handle fairly and equitably the power granted them in the interest of the whole people. There must be checks and balances in the law to guarantee that the power and the freedom granted to one segment of the people in the interest of all shall not be used arrogantly and selfishly. Inevitably—man being what he is—some newspaper publishers concluded that the power to publish as they pleased rested exclusively with them and not with the rights of the people. Consequently some of the newspapers, given the widest possible latitude in the interest of the people, became in their arrogance and selfishness the enemy of the people's right to see, hear, and read.

As a result, the people got, not a free press, but "yellow journalism," a phrase adapted from a comic picture series, "The Yellow Kid," published in William Randolph Hearst's newspapers. Yellow journalism, taking advantage of the privileges granted the press by the Constitution, gave the people—according to the *Encyclopaedia Britannica*—"(1) 'scare heads' in large type, printed in black or red; (2) lavish use of pictures; (3) pseudoscientific articles; (4) the Sunday supplement, with colored comics and sensational features;

(5) ostentatious crusading for popular causes." And, more seriously, while such newspapers were diverting the people in this way they were also perverting the people's religious, social and political views. Responsible historians in great numbers now conclude that the people of the United States were sucked into supporting the Spanish American War by jingoistic newspapers. The era of yellow journalism declined around the beginning of this century—largely under the influence of the *New York Times,* which was revived by Adolph S. Ochs and made a paper that correctly claimed to give "all the news that's fit to print." But, with some exceptions, the newspapers in the United States retain some of the marks of yellow journalism to this day.

To the extent that the press reports only deceptive fragments of daily events and conceals facts on which the welfare of the people depends, where there is no clearly distinguishable line between its report of the news and its editorial opinions, where arrogantly and callously the press defames and ruins men with false or unjust attacks on their character or profession, when it handles court cases in such a manner as to preclude the securing of justice, then the press becomes the enemy rather than the servant and ally of the people. And, when the press thus betrays those from whom its power and freedom derive, it abrogates its right to such freedom and power.

Depending on the seriousness of the press's offense against the people, the people have recourse to the correctives built into a competitive market and where necessary to the law. The freedom of the press should be zealously guarded; but wherever necessary the law should guarantee that the freedom of the press serve the right of the people to knowledge and to opinion. Therefore in our society the press, however careful we should be to protect its freedom, cannot be superior to the law, for it cannot be superior to the people whose Constitution authorizes and liberates the press.

What is true of the press in particular—newspapers—is true of the press in general—all forms of mass communication. In a day in which newspapers have a decreasing role in mass communication, it would be a threat to the people's freedom to deprive the electronic media of the privileges that have traditionally been enjoyed by newspapers. But it is the other side of this matter that concerns us here. If it is necessary to keep newspapers under the surveillance of the government for the protection of the people, it is likewise necessary to keep the new media of communication under government supervision.

Indeed, the argument that radio and television should be under stricter governmental control than newspapers and magazines has some justification in the fact that the medium through which they operate—the ether—belongs to the whole people. Despite the obvious differences between the slow media and the fast, we can lay down the general principle that the electronic media should have the maximum freedom consistent with the freedom of the people but that these media are not superior to the government of that people whose ether the media use and whom they are authorized to serve. There will be occasions when the pressure of the law must be applied to radio- and television-broadcasting to protect the rights of the people to that freedom that is the habitat of authentic morality. What are the circumstances under which we may be compelled to seek new laws or a stricter enforcement of laws that already exist to keep radio and television healthfully regulated?

In earlier chapters and in this one I have alluded to seven conditions under which the law should prevent the mass media's offending the rights of the people. Let us now list these conditions in summary form, touching not what might happen but dangers already threatening.

plan * First, the government has the right and the duty to protect children in their formative years against broadcasts that would have a traumatic effect on their highly impressionable lives. Obviously we can rely neither on the broadcasting industry nor on indolent parents to protect children in their years of greatest vulnerability to the dramatization of sexuality and violence. As was indicated in the chapter on censorship, this protection of children cannot be easily accomplished without endangering the freedom of adults to see and hear what they please. Indeed, there is no way to solve this problem completely. But the threat to children can be reduced by a rigid scheduling that eliminates lusty, adult programs from the normal viewing time of children. The argument that nationwide broadcasting makes such scheduling impossible does not hold water in a day when few entertainments are, or need to be, broadcast live.

Second, the law has a responsibility to the people whenever the broadcasting industry's preoccupation with profits deprives the people of high-quality public service programing. It has been presumed that the broadcasting industry owes the public non-commercial programs in religious, educational, and civic fields. Put more correctly, such programs are the right of a people who permit the broadcasting business to use their airwaves for commercial purposes. But public service broadcasting has eroded in recent years, partly because of the greed of the broadcasting industry and partly because of the indifference of those organizations—including the churches—that should have consumed every minute of available time but instead permitted the erosion to occur. A stricter enforcement of the law will correct one side of this problem; but religious, educational, and civic organizations must correct the other side of it.

Third, the people are deprived of high quality broadcasting by an increasing flood of advertisements that break up newscasts, sports, and drama into monotonous snippets. Occasional broadcasts by the Bell Telephone Company, the Xerox Company, Hallmark Cards, and others show us what television broadcasting can and should be, but there is a paucity of such programs. Increasingly, television broadcasting goes the way of radio broadcasting before it, as the amount of uninterrupted programing diminishes and the number of spot advertisements increases. Since, as we have seen, the public pays in one way or another for all broadcasting, the sharp increase in the number of commercials means that the people are paying more and more for less and less. Radio and television companies are in a category somewhat different from most public utilities; but the regulation of the broadcasting industries should be similar in guaranteeing that the people get their money's worth from a medium that employs the ether that belongs to the people.

Fourth, it is the duty of the government to guarantee that radio and television serve the needs, rights, and interests of all the people, equitably and indiscriminately. America's minorities—Negroes, Spanish Americans, and Indians—suffer inequities at the hands of the electronic mass media. It should be noted that the nationwide networks are making an earnest and increasingly successful effort to eliminate such discrimination. The fault lies with local stations such as the ones to which I have referred: WLBT-TV and WJTV in Jackson, Mississippi. In referring to or addressing Negroes these stations did not give them the common and elementary courtesies given whites. Although the case the United Church of Christ brought against these stations has not been finally resolved at the time of writing, the point made here is that it should be the government's duty to protect the broadcasting interests of minorities, that it should do so as routine policy, and that it should not be necessary for the minorities to go to the courts to receive basic American justice.

Fifth, the government should protect men and organizations against slander over radio and television much more zealously and effectively than it does. Here, too, the harm is done not by the networks but by local stations that sell time to hatemongers who scurrilously and irresponsibly attack their enemies. The victims may not even know that they are under attack or what is being said about them. In recent months the Federal Communication Commission has ruled that the station must notify those subjected to attack within a week or face a fine up to ten thousand dollars. (Carl McIntire, who broadcasts daily paid programs over an estimated six hundred radio stations, has incessantly condemned the F.C.C. for this ruling, claiming that his right to say what he pleases about people without their knowing it is in the American tradition of free speech.) The F.C.C. has moved in the right direction, but it is not enough for the stations to notify people that they have been or will be subjected to denunciation on a certain day, and to offer them equal time to reply. The defamers of character and reputation should be subject to serious penalty—as under the law they are—and the stations that carry their material should be viewed by the government as an accomplice in slander.

Sixth, federal laws should open the way to two kinds of television not now in existence on a national scale: Pay-TV and Public TV. I have already argued sufficiently in the chapter on the people's ether for both of these forms as additions to commercial TV, and I now stress the word "additions," because I do not consider either of these forms of broadcasting replacements of commercial television. Certainly I would be opposed to a government monopoly of television and would consider such a monopoly a danger to the people's freedom. But strictly regulated, sharply focused Public TV, operated by the government for specific and limited purposes, would remedy several of the ills now haunting American television.

Seventh, I see little improvement of radio and television in the directions I have indicated until two developments occur. First, the Federal Communications Commission must be required by the people's pressure to do what it is already empowered by the law to do. There is much that the F.C.C. could do that it is not now doing. The churches, I have said, can help stiffen the F.C.C.'s spine and make it active where it is now timidly inactive. Second, commercial television will never serve the best interest of the people as long as so many of the people's representatives in Washington retain immense personal investments in commercial radio and television. I have therefore suggested that the law require all public servants who have any influence over the fate of commercial broadcasting to divest themselves of all personal and family investments in commercial broadcasting. In such a crucial area of the nation's life as this one, public servants should not be subject to the conflicts of interest inevitable where they are financially involved in commercial broadcasting. They will be more likely to serve the public rather than themselves if they withdraw their investments from radio and television. I end this chapter with this suggestion, but the healing of the industry should begin with it.

10
Morality and the Sense of God's Presence

This concluding chapter could be titled an epilogue, for it breaks sharply with the practical issues I have been discussing in previous chapters and returns our thoughts to some of the theoretical issues with which this book began. Yet the purpose here is entirely practical, for its objective is to close the void many Christians permit to exist between faith and works, between the spiritual and the physical, and to do so finally in the mass media setting.

The truest, most precious, and at the same time most dangerous Christian doctrine holds that man's salvation is by grace through faith. To that doctrine I subscribe. But it tempts us to believe that since there is no saving merit in our works, morality becomes optional for those who believe. It encourages the conclusion that the whole round of religion can be lived within the brain and soul of the individual man and need not be concerned with what happens to man in a dirty, brutal world. It offers us consolation in saying "Lord, Lord" whether or not we do the will of Christ's Father in heaven. And, in regard to the dominant theme of this book, it asks why we should be concerned about the moral effects of mass media when the only thing necessary is to persuade men to profess faith in Jesus Christ.

We cannot afford to ignore the incontestable biblical evidence that God prefers the man who has his doubts about God but sincerely serves his fellowman to the one who says he loves God but feels under no divine obligation to his fellowman: "He who says 'I know him' but disobeys his commandments is a liar, and the truth is not in him; but whoever keeps his word, in him truly love for God is perfected" (1 John 2:4-5). And, of course, there is a needed corrective in James 2:17—"Faith by itself, if it has no works, is dead." What merit has our faith if we are indifferent to the good and the evil the mass media do to "these little ones"?

If we drift back into uncorrected definitions of morality, what I now say about morality and the sense of God's presence will be utterly confusing. Therefore let us begin this closing chapter with a sharp review of terms.

Authentic morality has its focus in people, its objective in the transforming of people into persons, its habitat in freedom, its criterion and energy in love, and its source in God. The manner in which I have put together the five parts of this definition may be original, but the parts themselves are not. They are found, indeed, in the writings of numerous twentieth-century theologians. And variants of this definition emerge in all centuries because it is rooted in the New Testament and specifically in that verse of the Scriptures that underlies this book like a text—John 10:10: "The thief comes only to steal and kill and destroy; I came that they may have life, and have it abundantly." So we have been asking in what way the mass media serve the thief and in what way they serve the giver of abundant life.

If this definition rather than legalism or relativism describes true morality, how is it related to our awareness of the presence of God? I will answer this question in three ways: first, by conceding that it is possible to participate in genuine morality without being a Christian or even a theist; second, by contending in John Macquarrie's words that "the moral life is in a very significant way illuminated by the Christian faith"; and third, by insisting that it is not possible to be a genuine Christian without participating in authentic morality. If these arguments are true, then the churches' task merely begins rather than ends when, through routine "conversions," they add new members to the Christian roster. In what way and to what extent do these new Christians participate in what God is doing in the world? How in their own lives and the lives of others do they help bring authentic man into being? In what special sense are the mass media their burden?

When we examine men's fruits we have to concede that the

morality of non-Christians often puts that of Christians to shame. This is true not only of non-Christian theists but also of an occasional atheist. The non-Christian but theistic believers know—as W. Adams Brown put it—that "the sense of God's presence, which is the crown of the religious life, reaches over into the sphere of ethics and glorifies it." All theists, however crude their concept of God, know that there is a better life and believe that in some way their God—or gods—delivers the secrets of that life to the faithful. Christianity has certainly produced its share, and more, of saintly men and women. But it would be risky history and fallacious theology to argue the superiority and the uniqueness of Christianity on the ground that it and it alone produces moral men. Even one exception would demolish that argument, and there have been many exceptions.

Likewise, atheists can participate in authentic morality. This does not mean that they can do so fully; it means only that atheists are not automatically barred from the broad ranges of genuine morality. They may not know the source of their concern that man become fully man or of the energy by which they give their lives to this end. (This is a part of their tragedy.) But the love and the power of the God they neither recognize nor acknowledge may nevertheless use them for his purposes. In the May 1, 1962, issue of *Presbyterian Life*, Robert McAfee Brown used a quotation from John Calvin which acknowledges that God can use all things—including heathens—for his purposes: "When, therefore, we meet with heathen writers, let us learn from that light of truth which is admirably displayed in their works, that the human mind, fallen as it is, and corrupted from its integrity, is yet invested and adorned by God with excellent talents. If we believe that the spirit of God is the only fountain of truth, we shall neither reject nor despise the truth itself, wherever it shall appear, unless we wish to insult the spirit of God."

How easily and correctly Calvin's words translate into an acknowledgment of God's power to use for his purposes in the world men who neither respect nor know him. If we believe—to paraphrase Calvin—that the spirit of God is the only fountain of morality, we shall neither reject nor despise morality itself, wherever it shall appear, unless we wish to insult the spirit of God. For the point is not to prove one human being morally superior to another but to rejoice wherever morality appears. Wherever there exists in Christian or non-Christian, in theist or atheist, a loving concern that people shall have the fullest opportunity to become persons, to unfold all the possibilities God has planted in them, there the will of God is done, whether those who do it acknowledge him or not. If God accepts and uses the morality of those who ignore him, who are we to spurn it?

Yet, however true it may be that every man, whatever the state of his theology, can participate in authentic morality, the Christian claims that the moral life is especially illuminated by the Christian faith. I am well aware of the peril of saying this, the danger of being dismissed as a presumptuous, arrogant bigot. But the Christian must run this risk if he accepts the Scriptures' designation of his Lord as uniquely and radically different from all other men.

In New Delhi, India, there is a beautiful modern temple built by the wealthy Birla family. It is dedicated to Hinduism and its derivative religions, Buddhism and Sikhism. Within this temple's marble walls there is an inscription that reads: "Dedicated to the only true religion: Hinduism, Buddhism, Sikhism, et cetera." Many Orientals can indulge in this kind of gracious inclusiveness, but the Christian cannot. His religion cannot be subsumed with others in anybody's "et cetera." However great other holy men may have been, the dissimilarity between them and the Christ is one not merely of degree but also of kind. The Christ is not merely a star of greater magnitude in a constellation of similar stars but is the light itself and that light, falling on general morality, transforms it into Christian morality.

I made this point as well as I can make it in a sermon preached at the University of Chicago Rockefeller Chapel shortly after I returned from the Third Assembly of the World Council of Churches in New Delhi, in 1961, a sermon published in *Rockefeller Chapel Sermons:*

The brilliant Hindu intellectual and vice-president of India, Radhakrishnan, has said, "Christians are an ordinary people who make extraordinary claims." Exactly. He meant it partly in derision, but it describes perfectly what we are. We are ordinary people. To approach the non-Christian world believing anything else, posing as anything else, is to validate their charge that we are bigots. Our faith makes us superior to no people, and our failure to keep the terms of that faith makes us inferior to no people. . . . Yes, we make extraordinary claims. We claim, as the Scriptures do, that Jesus Christ is *the* Light of the world, incomparable, irreplaceable, essential. We claim that he is brother to every man, yet utterly different from any man. We claim that in him and in him alone the fullness of the eternal Word of God became flesh and dwelt among us. We claim that at his name every knee should bow and every tongue confess that he is Lord. We make extraordinary claims, not for ourselves—God forbid that we should make claims for ourselves—but for that one who wills to be the Savior of all men and who, whether all men know it or not, is their Lord. . . . There is a radical difference between light and darkness, however dim the light, however deep the darkness. We therefore welcome all lights and respect them wherever they shine. . . . But there is also a radical difference between lights and *the* light, between God's sons and his Son, between holy men and Jesus Christ.

Christianity—like other religions—claims that it is the imperial religion, that its Christ is *the* Light of the world. This is the light that for Christians illuminates authentic morality.

The Christian—if he is genuinely Christian—is under the specific orders of his Lord, in word and example, to make people the focus of his life. He has seen in Jesus Christ the image of the true man, the person into whom God wills to transform people. The Christian knows the dimensions of true freedom, for in Christ he has received the truth that makes men free. In Christ he has received the love that tests and enables true morality. And in Christ he has seen the God who is the source of his morality and that of all men. Does this describe the life of every man who bears the name of Jesus Christ? Indeed not. Does it describe the potential of every man who is in Christ? Indeed so.

We have seen that it is possible to participate in genuine morality without being a Christian or a theist and, nevertheless, that the Christian faith illuminates and enriches the moral life in a significant way. The third assertion about the relation of a sense of God's presence to morality is that the genuine Christian must participate in authentic morality or cease being a Christian. This could not be said if we were defining morality in old terms as good deeds or as personal piety; but it must be said when we give morality the broader and deeper definition. The Christian is no Christian if he does not gladly participate in what God is doing in the world. And, to repeat, what God seeks in the world is to bring his children into the fulness of that manhood revealed in Christ. Since this is plainly God's purpose in the world, since it is the work to which he calls his people, since it is the cause for which he sent and sacrificed his Son, no man who spurns this divine enterprise merits the name of Christ. Let us examine this assertion more closely and see what follows.

Where evangelism is separated from authentic morality, where the "winning of men to Christ" does not include winning them to a personal engagement in enabling people to become persons, evangelism becomes a deceptive and meaningless ritual. Indeed, an evangelism that merely urges men to profess faith in Christ without telling them what it means to live in Christ is both dishonest and dangerous. Any child old enough to become a professing Christian—or in some churches a "confirmed" Christian—is old enough to understand the basic dimensions of the Christian life. To lure a child or an adult into Christ's family without telling him plainly what is expected of him as a Christian, without introducing him to the essentials of Christian morality, defrauds him, however good the intention. Indeed we have too often made profession of faith in Christ the parroting of a cliché rather than a total commitment.

Where there is no authentic morality there is no genuine ministry. There are numerous clergymen who believe that their specialized professional roles justify their leaving to others Christ's dirty, painful tasks in the world. There are lay churchmen who believe that being a good father, an honest businessman, or a loyal supporter of the church relieves them of any Christian duty to be Christ's representative "where the action is," where the most pressing problems appear in the world. These views are false. It is possible for ministers and laymen to perform their obligation to the church without discharging their duty to the Christ. Indeed, under some circumstances it happens that faithfulness to the church becomes our apology for not serving Christ in the world. Unless, in Robert L. Holmes's words, a man "address himself with all the power of his conviction to the most pressing problems of the day," he is failing his duty to his Christ.

Where there is no authentic morality, genuine worship diminishes. I am not suggesting that the absence of an authentically moral life eliminates genuine worship entirely. God is always available to all men, always waiting for them and seeking them, always searching for those who need him most, always pleased when men sincerely praise him. And those who need him most are those most deeply estranged from their fellowmen. Nevertheless it would appear from the Scriptures that there are human duties that have priority over worship and that, when unfulfilled, cripple worship. In the Sermon on the Mount, Jesus said: "If you are offering your gift at the altar, and there remember that your brother has something against you, leave your gift there before the altar and go; first be reconciled to your brother, and then come and offer your gift." As Sherman E. Johnson said in his exegesis of the Gospel of Matthew in *The Interpreter's Bible,* "It is idle for a man to try to maintain right relations with God through worship if he is not at peace with his neighbor." How much of our worship, then, rises no higher than the church ceiling?

It is likewise true that private worship—what we sometimes call "private devotions"—diminishes where there is no authentic morality. Unfortunately, the phrase "private devotions" suggests not only that a man can have a personal encounter with God but also that he can shut the whole world out when he does so. The desire for absolute privacy in the presence of God—a mental as well as a physical privacy—is a travesty against the oneness we have in Christ and, more than that, it is a psychological impossibility. Leo Tolstoy used to play with his young children a game in which he would send them behind a door, telling them that the first one to think of a big, black bear would have to come out and lose the game. Obviously these games were of short duration. The children immediately remembered what they had been ordered to forget. Likewise if we enter our closets determined to think only of God and ourselves, we cannot long remain there successful in our exclusiveness. Where there is no authentic morality, private worship diminishes.

From these illustrations it should be evident that the moral life of a Christian and his spiritual life are inseparable and that he must meet the mass media's challenge to morality with his whole being.

The first chapter of this book began with the question as to "what way and to what extent mass media affect morality." This has been a dominant theme throughout these pages, but underlying it, and surfacing frequently, has been a second question no less crucial, no less decisive. For we have been asking in what way and to what extent Christian morality can be brought to bear on the mass media so as to make them conducive to the fulness of human life.

The first question is important and the first task is imperative, for—in Paul's words to the Romans—we must "not be overcome by evil." Nor, if we can prevent it, should Christians permit their culture to be overcome by the demoralization we have discovered in the mass media. We have discovered aspects of the mass media to which we must say as effective a no as we can, even to the extent of using the state's power under circumstances we have clearly defined and limited.

Yet, if we Christians are consumed by the first question and exhausted by the first task we shall find ourselves fighting a defensive battle we cannot win. If we merely condemn what is bad in the mass media, arrogantly demanding that the media eliminate what we condemn, and at the same time fail to offer the media creative alternatives to what we condemn, then no one will pay attention to our criticism and no one should.

In the second clause of Paul's admonition to the Romans there is wisdom we should not ignore: "Overcome evil with good." Since in one form or another the electronic media of communication are here to stay, it is the duty of Christians to preserve and support them wherever they serve authentic morality and to woo and instruct them wherever the communication industry defaults its duty to the people. There are occasions in which the Christian strategy will require that Christians deprive some radio and television stations of their licenses if they can. But in most cases it is far better to redeem the stations than to destroy them. Redemption, after all, is the Christian enterprise.

But deeper still there is for Christians who are concerned about morality and the mass media a third question and a third task underlying all of our concerns for the world. The question is this: What is the character of the people with whom the churches and Christian homes are confronting the mass media? And the task is this: We must examine and test not only the mass media but ourselves, not only the effect of mass media on our children but the effect of our teaching and our example on our children, not only what the churches can do to redeem the mass media but what the churches must do to be redeemed themselves. If this task were perfectly performed, that would not solve the problem posed by the mass media. But if the churches and Christian homes were performing their first duty, the problems posed by the mass media would greatly diminish.